REVOLUTION AND
COUNTER-REVOLUTION
IN IRAN

This book is published with the aid of the **Bookmarks Publishing Co-operative**. Many socialists have some savings put aside, probably in a bank or savings bank. While it is there, this money is being loaned out by the bank to some business or other to further the capitalist search for profit. We believe it is better loaned to a socialist venture to further the struggle for socialism. That's how the co-operative works: in return for a loan, repayable at a month's notice, members receive free copies of books published by Bookmarks. At the time this book was published, the co-operative had more than 250 members, from as far apart as London Malaysia, Canada and Norway.

Like to know more? Write to **Bookmarks Publishing Co-operative**, 265 Seven Sisters Road, Finsbury Park, London N4 2DE, England.

REVOLUTION AND COUNTER-REVOLUTION IN IRAN

PHIL MARSHALL

BOOKMARKS
London, Chicago and Melbourne

Revolution and Counter-revolution in Iran
by Phil Marshall

Published April 1988
Bookmarks, 265 Seven Sisters Road, London N4 2DE, England
Bookmarks, PO Box 16085, Chicago, IL 60616, USA
Bookmarks, GPO Box 1473N, Melbourne 3001, Australia
Copyright © Bookmarks and Phil Marshall

ISBN 0 906224 43 8

Printed by Cox and Wyman, Reading, England
Typeset by Artworkers, London
Design by Peter Court

Bookmarks is linked to an international grouping of
    socialist organisations:
AUSTRALIA: **International Socialists**, GPO Box
    1473N, Melbourne 3001.
BELGIUM: **Socialisme International**, 9 rue Marexhe,
    4400 Herstal, Liege
BRITAIN: **Socialist Workers Party**, PO Box 82,
    London E3.
CANADA: **International Socialists**, PO Box 339,
    Station E, Toronto, Ontario M6H 4E3
DENMARK: **Internationale Socialister**, Morten
    Borupsgade 18, kld, 8000 Arhus C.
FRANCE: **Socialisme International** (correspondence to
    Yves Coleman, BP 407, Paris Cedex 05).
IRELAND: **Socialist Workers Movement**,
    PO Box 1648, Dublin 8.
NORWAY: **Internasjonale Sosialister**, Postboks 5370
    Majorstua, 0304 Oslo 3.
UNITED STATES: **International Socialist
    Organization**, PO Box 16085, Chicago, IL 60616.
WEST GERMANY: **Sozialistische Arbeiter Gruppe**,
    Wolfgangstrasse 81, 6000 Frankfurt 1.

Contents

GLOSSARY OF ARABIC AND FARSI TERMS

anjoman-e islami: islamic society

ayatollah: senior religious leader

baseej: mobilisation

bazaar: institution based on the market-place, comprising stallholders, artisans, merchants, financiers

fatwa: religious decree

fedai (plural *fedayeen*): self-sacrificer

hezbollah: party of Allah

hezbollahi: member of the party of Allah, supporter of the Khomeini regime

homafar: airman

imam: prayer leader, religious leader

jahad: crusade, holy war

jahad-e sazandegi: reconstruction crusade

komiteh: neighbourhood committee

majlis: assembly, parliament

maktabi: committed Muslim, one who is correct

mojahed (plural *mojahedin*): volunteer for *jahad*, combatant

mostakberin: oppressor

mostazafin: needy, oppressed

mullah: low-ranking cleric

pasdar (plural *pasdaran*): guard

paykar: combat

savak (acronym): secret police of the Pahlavi regime

shah: king

sharia: islamic law

shora: council

taqiyya: dissimulation, concealing the truth

tudeh: masses

ulema: body of religious scholars

umma: nation, community

waqf: religious endowment

Introduction

IT IS almost ten years since the Iranian revolution and still many socialists are at a loss to explain the events of that great mass movement. In Iran and around the world some talk enthusiastically of the 'Islamic' revolution, of the positive role of the religious leadership and today's 'progressive' government. Others look at the repression practised by the Khomeini regime and conclude that the whole experience was a catastrophe. For some, Iran has advanced towards a form of 'popular power'; for others, it has regressed to forms worse than those of the Shah's Pahlavi dynasty. For some, Khomeini is a strong anti-imperialist leader; for others, he is a butcher.

The picture is complicated by the Gulf War. With the West lining up behind Iraq and using its military might against Iran, socialists in the Western countries have been the first to defend Iran against a new imperialist threat. But does this mean they should look favourably on the Khomeini regime – and does the Gulf conflict mean that socialists in Iran should be less critical of their rulers? These questions can only be answered if we can understand the revolution and the character of the society it produced.

The revolution which removed the Shah in 1979 was of immense importance. It raised every key question in the Marxist tradition: the nature of imperialism; the fragility of capitalism in crisis; the role of the working class; the power of the state; the questions of ideology and religion, of nationalities, of women's liberation; above all, the question of the character of the revolutionary workers' party. Yet just as there is disagreement on the character of today's Iran, there is continuing dispute about each of these questions.

This book looks at the revolution in order to clarify these problems, allowing revolutionaries to add the Iranian experience to the fund of knowledge on which all international socialists must draw. It is also written in the belief that understanding the revolution is the first step towards the building of a healthy socialist current within Iran.

Author's acknowledgement
Thanks to the friends and comrades whose advice and criticism have helped in the writing of this book: Colin Barker, Alex Callinicos, Tony Cliff, Ali Hassani, Clare Hill, Charlie Hore, Mansour Mansouri, Peter Marsden, Maryam Poya, John Rose and Farhang Tabrizi.

Phil Marshall writes on the Middle East for **International Socialism** and **Socialist Worker Review**. He is a member of the Socialist Workers Party in Britain.

1: Capitalism in Iran

WHEN the Shah's regime fell in February 1979, Iran's religious leaders proclaimed the success of an 'Islamic revolution'. They claimed that victory had been achieved through the efforts of millions of pious Muslims acting under the direction of the religious establishment. This was to be the first great myth of the revolution and one that has since obscured most attempts to understand it.

The refrain was taken up by many Iranians, including sections of the left, while abroad, theories of 'revolutionary Islam' began to flourish. Academics in the West discovered new virtues in the traditions of Shia Islam and some attempted syntheses of Marxism and religion on the basis of the Iranian experience.[1]

But the roots of the revolution did not lie in the history of Shiism or the special character of Iran's religious institutions. They lay in the changes taking place in Iranian capitalism.

The forces that made the revolution were the product of years of capitalist development. This history has itself been obscured – partly as a result of years of propaganda from the Pahlavi dictatorship. But socialists, too, have misunderstood much of Iranian history because of the theoretical distortions built into their views of development. As we shall see, these were to lead the left to construct a false picture of Iranian society and to pursue strategies which led them to disaster.

What, then, are the key features of modern Iranian history – and what implications do they have for socialist practice?

The beginnings of capitalism

For most of the Iranian left the decisive period in the development of Iranian capitalism has been the past 30 years.[2] In fact, the Iranian system has been shaped by forces that began to emerge almost 100 years ago.

In the 1880s Iran was on the margin of the world economy. Of a population estimated at 9.9 million, the great majority lived in the countryside; 90 per cent of the workforce was dependent upon agriculture and a nomadic lifestyle. Huge areas of land were held by absentee landlords, while most of the rural population was landless. Less than a million people lived in the cities, where a merchant class and a layer of small traders and *bazaaris*[3] exercised some influence. A weak government ruled in the name of the Shah, who effectively represented the landed interests.

According to a widely-held view, there was no domestic industry and no indigenous capitalist class. In fact an embryonic industrial bourgeoisie was already in existence. For much of the nineteenth century Iranian entrepreneurs had organised the production of textiles and silks, mainly for the Western market. In mid-century, competition from cheaper products, especially from Britain and Russia, began to force these goods out of the international market, causing the collapse of sections of the industry. But by the 1870s increased demand from the West for carpets and the finer textiles had produced renewed activity. Both 'cottage' industry and workshop production developed and the position of the merchants and entrepreneurs was strengthened.[4]

As part of the effort to reinforce their own position, the Shahs tried to speed up this process. They hoped to benefit from increased revenue from new industries, which they believed could best be established by inviting foreign investment. In 1872 the Shah granted a concession to the British businessman Baron de Reuter, later of news agency fame, effectively giving him rights to exploit all Iran's resources. Like most such attempts during this period, the Reuters concession failed to establish new industries, but it caused great resentment among the merchant class. When, in 1890, the Shah granted a monopoly on the production, sale and export of tobacco to another British businessman, a mass opposition movement erupted. Under the leadership of the merchants and with strong backing from religious leaders, the Shah was forced to back down. The pace of economic change was slow – but already it was being reflected in political upheaval.

By the turn of the century the most modern sectors of the economy were shared between foreign capitalists and the small domestic bourgeoisie. The telegraph company, the fishing industry of the Caspian Sea and the main road construction company were operated by foreign concessionaries. However, domestic capital was consolidating and controlled most industrial production. The bulk of manufactured goods were produced by artisans in a host of tiny workshops, but there were small factories in the carpet-weaving and leather industries and a number of mines and printshops. According to one study of the period, the largest workplace was a Tabriz carpet factory with 1,500 workers.[5]

Between 1900 and 1914 development speeded up. Thirty modern factories were established, some through further sale of concessions, others through the extension of Iranian merchant capital into industrial production. The government attempted to stimulate further investment – again with an eye to increasing its revenues – and established a ministry of public utilities which encouraged foreign and Iranian capital alike. Merchants established a number of companies on the Western joint-stock basis, selling shares to other merchants, entrepreneurs, landowners, government officials and members of the ruling family. Religious leaders played a leading role in persuading Iranians to invest in some projects, declaring it a holy cause to support companies which aimed to encourage Iranian manufacturing and eliminate Western products from the market.[6]

While only a fraction of economic activity was in manufacturing, the sector had consolidated. One recent study of economic development at this period concludes:

> Notwithstanding the many obstacles modern industry had to overcome in Iran – cost of raw materials, energy, high transport rates, no protection against foreign competition and non-economic factors – industrialisation both prior to and after 1900 until World War One was considerable.[7]

The changes were soon reflected in political developments. Opposition to the Shah's efforts to introduce foreign capital stimulated the Constitutional Revolution of 1905, in which a mass movement again threatened the monarchy. It was led by an unstable alliance of the merchant class, religious leaders, the modernising professionals and intelligentsia and the embryonic bourgeoisie. The monarchy was forced to concede a constitution in which bourgeois democratic rights – free speech, free association and free assembly – were granted and the merchants and bourgeoisie allowed some rights of representation in a *majlis* (parliament).

Economic and political change had an impact in other areas of society. The small working class had been growing steadily, and encouraged by the freedoms granted in the revolution, workers' organisations began to emerge. The first reliably-recorded strike in Iran took place in November 1906, among fishermen in Enzeli employed by the Russian company Liazonov, one of the few successful foreign concessions.[8] In 1907 telegraphists in Tabriz and Tehran, dockers and sailors in Enzeli, and printers, electricity and tram workers in Tabriz were involved in strikes, demanding increased wages, shorter hours, paid holidays and improved working conditions.[9] Trade unions were established: first among printers in Tehran, then among dockers and boatmen, shoemakers, tram drivers and carpet weavers.[10]

An important development had taken place: while the monarchist faction of the ruling class had been frustrated in its efforts to force the pace of national development, a small modern sector had emerged. This was on a modest scale and confined to a handful of cities. Nevertheless, the class antagonisms characteristic of capitalist relations of production were becoming evident; an embryonic bourgeoisie and a tiny proletariat were already in conflict.

Consolidation of capitalism

In 1908 oil was discovered in the south-western province of Khuzistan. The rapid development of an integrated modern industrial sector followed, as oil companies brought in equipment and began a programme of construction. This coincided with the establishment of the first railways, and together the two projects provided the basis for the first large concentrations of workers employed within Iran. (Migrants from the north had formed the first group of Iranian workers in the oilfields of Russia.[11]

During this period there were further efforts to force the pace of industrialisation, notably the government's invitation to an American mission to oversee development. But the First World War brought invasion by the armies of Britain, France and Russia, slowing up the whole process.

After the war Iran was in a state of great instability. Central government had become weaker, allowing the development of regional movements in the northern provinces of Gilan and Azerbaijan. In the cities, the population had been radicalised by the experience of foreign occupation and the success of the October 1917 revolution in Russia. Workers in industries with an earlier tradition of organisation – notably the printers and bakers – led a new wave of struggles, while there were the first strikes in the oil industry.[12] By 1921 the unions claimed 20,000 members in an industrial workforce estimated at 100,000.[13] By November 1921 the movement had gained such strength that, under the influence of the newly-formed Communist Party of Iran, a central Union Council was formed, which affiliated to the Profintern – the Red International of Labour Unions established by the Communist International.[14]

Despite the small size of the working class the level of struggle was high. In 1921, the bakers, printers, postal workers, dockers, oil workers, tailors and teachers went on strike – the last of these in protest against a decree that no government official might join a union.[15] Further successful strikes followed in 1923 but in the summer of that year the whole movement abruptly went into decline as the army launched a campaign of repression.

The campaign was initiated by Reza Khan, who, backed by Britain, had seized control of the army. His republican rhetoric expressed the anxieties of the increasingly-important merchant class and the bourgeoisie. Dissatisfied with a weak Shah – whom Reza Khan expelled in 1920 – and afraid of the regional movements and workers' organisations, these classes looked to the leader of a modernised army to restore state control. They were the first beneficiaries of his attacks on the regional movements in Gilan, Kurdistan and Khurasan and on the workers' movement.

By 1925 Reza Khan was strong enough to abandon republicanism and declare himself Shah. However, he adopted a modernisation programme closely fitting the needs of the bourgeoisie, which was demanding state investment and protection for local industry, and introduced the country's first effective development strategy.

Efforts to provide Iran with a modern infrastructure were combined with a major programme of industrialisation. Reza Shah did not look outside the country for capital, as his predecessors had done, but financed state activity by using oil revenues and large sums raised through taxation. Meanwhile he encouraged merchants and factory-owners to step up investment. The system of privileges for foreign states was abolished, Iranian financial institutions established and a policy of import substitution introduced. High tariff barriers protected local industries – a vital consideration as recession hit the world economy.

The state was the main agency of change but in an often-neglected development the bourgeoisie and merchant class played important roles. Together, state and private capital made the expansion of industrial capital a largely Iranian effort.

A recent history of financial development in Iran comments that at the state level,

> Considerable emphasis was placed on the fact that this growth was financed by the Iranians themselves. Offers of foreign loans were turned down, and with oil revenues largely allocated to military purposes by the mid-1930s, the cost of the development programme rested on taxes, mainly on consumption, together with an increase in the money supply.[16]

Meanwhile, among the bourgeoisie and the merchant class there was 'investment fever'. With profits of 60-80 per cent commonly returned from new industrial projects, the bourgeoisie grew more and more confident. A British report of 1936 described the effect in Azerbaijan:

> Even those who in the face of diminished opportunities for investment in private trade were disposed to hoard their capital, are now being persuaded by the success so far of certain pioneer factories, and their inability to convert funds into safer foreign currencies, to participate in industrial developments.[17]

In Isfahan, it was said, 'Nearly every section of the population has invested some, if not all, of its savings.'[18]

The results were dramatic: there was a wave of industrialisation, which by 1931 saw the establishment of 30 large factories and 200 smaller plants, mainly in textiles, foodstuffs and construction materials.[19] Growth continued for almost ten years; by 1941 there were 346 modern plants and a total of $260 million had been placed in industry – a strikingly large sum for a country often regarded as entirely undeveloped at this period.[20]

The main effect of the development programme was to strengthen the state, but the bourgeoisie also profited greatly. Reza Shah did not incorporate either merchants or industrial capitalists at the higher levels of the political system, preferring to consolidate the power of loyal sections of the landowning class. But the 20 years after his accession were a vital period of growth for Iranian capital, which pocketed large sums and, more importantly, saw its place in the Iranian economic system guaranteed.

During thhe same period the working class grew rapidly. According to one estimate, the number of industrial workers increased by 250 per cent between the mid-1920s and mid-1930s; another suggests a 250 per cent increase between 1934 and 1938.[21] Figures for the number of workers vary widely – from 170,000 to 261,000 and even 525,000 by 1940.[22]

Most workers were still employed in small workshops but the numbers in large plants had increased steadily. By 1940, 11 factories employed between 1,000 and 2,000 workers and another 17 between 500 and 1,000.[23] There were eight large textile mills in Isfahan, employing a total of 5,372 workers; two in Yazd (1,074), one in Kerman (696), and one in Shahi (3,396). In Tehran there were four tanneries employing a total of 5,000 workers. [24] In the oil industry the workforce had grown to more than 30,000; on the railways to 14,000; and in construction and road-building to 60,000.[25]

Trade union activities had declined sharply after the repression of the mid-1920s and remained at a relatively low level throughout the period of industrial development. Organisation did take place in a number of industries – producing strikes on the railways in Mazanderan in 1928, in the Abadan oil refinery in 1929, the Tabriz match industry and the Isfahan textile industry in 1930. Thereafter, for the rest of Reza Shah's rule, the unions were wholly ineffective.

The decline of workers' organisation had much to do with the regime imposed by the Shah's police, but demoralisation among activists who were members or supporters of the Communist Party of Iran (CPI) played a part. During the late 1920s the Communist International, to which the party was affiliated, lurched from one strategy to another in response to the needs of Moscow's foreign policy. The CPI loyally pursued the Moscow line but by 1929 found itself abandoned – Stalin's regime had decided to secure a closer relationship with Reza Shah and instructed its embassy in Tehran to break off all relations with the party, which soon collapsed. This destroyed, at a stroke, the remaining network of militants who had led the movement of the early 1920s.

Oil

Following the discovery of oil in 1908 a concession had been acquired by the Anglo-Persian Oil Company (APOC), which by 1911 was pumping oil for export and by 1913 had built a major service complex and a refinery at Abadan. APOC worked as an arm of British imperial policy: the British government held a 51 per cent stake and viewed the Khuzistan oilfields as its own. APOC operated the area as an enclave, wholly separated from the rest of the Iranian economy. So great was the dislocation between the oil-producing areas and the rest of Iran that, until the 1930s, most of Iran's demand for refined oil products was met by imports from Russia.

The scale of the pillage of Iranian oil by the British was staggering: between 1912 and 1933 APOC made profits of £200 million, of which only £16 million was paid to the Iranian government in direct royalties.[26] But the flow of capital to the Shah was still enough, in a backward country, to dictate that Iran should begin to take on the character of a *rentier* state – one in which the ruling group received much of its income from the sale of the country's resources. By the mid-1920s, direct royalties represented about 10 per cent of the government's budget, and by the early 1930s, about 30 per cent.[27]

Oil did not directly stimulate new industries. Most of APOC's needs, including building materials and even food and clothing, were imported. However, over the course of 30 years it did play a role in helping to establish a new industrial base. During the 1920s and 1930s direct oil revenues accounted for up to 30 per cent of visible imports and while much went to finance the Shah's militarisation programme, a small but important portion provided foreign exchange to equip the new manufacturing plants.

The oil industry also became one of the country's principal employers. While oil was not labour-intensive, the scale of Iranian production was such that by 1920 it was employing 20,000 workers and by 1940, 31,500 workers – one of the largest concentrations of workers in the Middle East.[28]

Combined and uneven development

By the Second World War Iran had experienced a series of attempts at development, in which the more ambitious sections of its ruling class had struggled to modernise the economy, mainly on the basis of introducing new industries. To the extent that Iran remained overwhelmingly backward and a subordinate state in the world system, their efforts had failed.

The country had at first been peripheral to world capitalism. When it became a vital energy source it remained subject to an extremely limited form of development – Britain being determined to secure oil but without any intention of stimulating wider development in a country which possessed no other resources of great interest. As a result, the oil installations became islands of advanced industry in Khuzistan, an area which had not changed in centuries.

Oil dominated the economy – but not to the exclusion of Iranian capital. While imperialism had pillaged Iran, it had not left the country undeveloped. The tiny industrial bourgeoisie of the early 1900s had been boosted by Iran's integration into the world system. Industrial capital still did not dominate commercial capital – even by 1940 far more was invested in commercial operations than in industry[29] – but industry had advanced, with the result that the uneven pattern of development produced in the oil province of Khuzistan was repeated elsewhere. Centres of modern production dotted the country. They were limited to the major cities – Tehran, Tabriz, Isfahan and a handful of other centres – but were industries in Iranian hands which used advanced techniques and employed substantial numbers of workers.

Iran was not advancing towards industrialisation on the same basis that the early capitalist countries, such as Britain and the US, had been transformed. No mass of entrepreneurs was forcing the pace of development, turning villages into industrial centres, making millions of peasants into proletarians – the domination of the industrialised countries over the world economy prevented such changes taking place at the edge of the system. Rather, a small, weak bourgeoisie was struggling to its feet, encouraged by a state with which it had a close but uncertain relationship. In short, the process of combined and uneven development was at work.[30]

This meant that despite the limited nature of the advanced sector of the economy, it produced the social forms associated with capitalism worldwide. Already the clash between capital and labour was an important characteristic of urban life. Development was producing a more unstable society, one in which the bourgeoisie was becoming more ambitious and the working class more conscious of its ability to act collectively. Reza Shah's attack on the mass movement during the 1920s slowed the workers' advance, but his policies of development subsequently deepened the contradictions in Iranian society. These contradictions were soon to surface anew.

The new workers' movement

The Second World War marked the end of the period of political consolidation Reza Shah had initiated in the 1920s. It ushered in more than ten years of mass struggles, culminating in a movement in which Iranian workers pushed the system to the brink of collapse.

In the mid-1930s the Shah had become frustrated by the limits placed on Iran's development by Britain and had turned to Germany, whose rulers had ambitions of their own in the region. By the late 1930s, more than half Iran's foreign trade was with

Germany, which provided much of the machinery for Iran's industrialisation programme.[31] This relationship caused Iran problems from the outbreak of world war in 1939 and in 1941 Britain and Russia invaded, with Britain intent on securing its oil interests in Khuzistan. The occupation armies soon replaced Reza Shah, by putting his son on the throne.

Occupation brought the development programme to an abrupt halt and much of manufacturing industry went into decline. However, the presence of foreign troops increased activity in the construction, transport and supply industries, while the oil industry – vital to Britain's war effort – received another boost. Merchants and petit bourgeois serving the occupation forces profited and the working class grew. At the same time, Britain and Russia relaxed the Shah's repressive regime, releasing political prisoners and allowing freedom to the press and to political parties.

The new freedoms did much to restore workers' self-confidence, and when faced with food shortages and an attempt to cut wages, they responded with a new wave of struggles. In 1942 there were strikes in the coalfields of Shamshak, and in Chalus and Sari workers occupied the textile mills and formed new unions.[32] In the larger industrial centres such as Tehran, Tabriz and Isfahan, survivors of the early labour movement returned to the factories and workshops to establish new organisations.

Some leading militants came from the Tudeh ('Masses') Party, formed in 1941 by a small group of leftists. This had few links with the Communist Party, which had collapsed in the late 1920s. It did not declare itself 'communist' but adopted a reform programme with which it hoped to attract 'workers, peasants, women and such members of the middle class as intellectuals, small landowners, craftsmen-traders and low-ranking government employees'.[33] It soon found that in the power vacuum created by occupation it was an important pole of attraction for intellectuals and worker militants. Tudeh members played a key role in developing the new union organisation, though by no means all worker activists were associated with the party.

A steady increase in militancy was evident from 1942, when there were 30 strikes. This total would have been higher had not the Tudeh held back its members, in order, it said, not to undermine the war effort – a response to pressures from Moscow. At this stage the party also refrained from organising in the oilfields, describing strikes at Kermanshah in 1943 as 'pro-fascist sabotage'.[34] The number of strikes rose to over 60 in 1944, as the key industrial centres joined the movement – in Tabriz, for example, workers in 16 of the city's 18 major plants joined strikes. By 1946 the annual number of strikes had risen to 183, disputes taking place mainly in the oil, construction, textile and leather industries. As the movement grew in confidence the scale of the strikes became greater: in Isfahan 20,000 textile workers joined a 1944 dispute, while in 1946 there were two mass strikes of the Khuzistan oil workers.[35]

The period after the First World War had seen the re-emergence of the unions; that following the Second World War now saw a similar development but on a far greater scale. By 1945 a new union federation under the leadership of the Tudeh claimed a membership of 275,000, and by 1946, when there were 186 affiliated unions, 335,000 members.[36] At the height of its power in August 1946, the United Central Council of the Unified Trade Unions of Iranian Workers (CCFTU) claimed 90,000 workers in the oilfields, 50,000 in each of the manufacturing centres of Tabriz and Tehran, 65,000 in the textile mills of Isfahan, Shiraz and Yazd, and 45,000 in the mills, coalfields and railways of Gilan and Mazanderan. This represented 75 per cent of the industrial labour force, with branches in almost every one of the country's modern plants. The explosion of union organisation in core industries affected workers in the most peripheral sectors of the economy – waiters and even cinema attendants were organised and union consciousness spread into the *bazaar* workshops.

The movement became the most important influence in national politics, notably when, after a three-day strike in 1946, 65,000 oil workers won most of their demands for increased pay and improved conditions. This symbolic struggle involved almost all the oil workers in Khuzistan and 15,000 non-oil workers in the province, including textile workers, *bazaar* craftsmen and road sweepers. It was the largest strike to have taken place in Iran and one of the largest in the Middle East, and showed that the barriers between workers in different workplaces and in different industries were breaking down. A sense of class solidarity was spreading among workers whom, only ten years earlier, had not dared raise their heads.

The declaration of autonomous, Russian-backed republics in Azerbaijan and Kurdistan deepened the government's sense of insecurity. Under pressure from the national movements and the tide of workers' struggles, it took in three Tudeh ministers and conceded a series of measures to the unions. These included a minimum wage, a 48-hour working week, voluntary overtime, limits to child labour, paid maternity leave, union rights and the establishment of joint factory councils representing labour and management – gains undreamt of in other countries of the region and, indeed, in many of the advanced industrial countries. Such was the pressure from below that a landlord-led government even issued a decree stipulating that landlords should give 15 per cent of the share of the crop to their peasants. [37]

The situation was becoming highly unstable. In the oilfields, the unions had been spectacularly successful and the Tudeh was effectively running affairs in the workplaces and urban centres. The British ambassador reported that 'at the present time the security of the refinery and the fields, and the safety of the British personnel, depends on the goodwill and pleasure of the Tudeh Party'.[38]

The government, with British backing, started a counter-offensive. The Tudeh ministers were dismissed, while British troops were sent to Basra in Iraq, close to the Khuzistan oilfields. Soon British-supported tribal forces were raiding Khuzistan and starting to rally tribal leaders, religious leaders and landlords against the Tudeh. Meanwhile union militants and party activists were arrested and there was a nationwide crackdown on Tudeh offices and clubs. A general strike in Tehran could not halt the offensive and by the end of 1946 the government had gained the upper hand.

The CCFTU now went into decline. This was not only the result of the ruling-class offensive but of the easing of some economic pressures and a rise in unemployment in some key areas as a result of the withdrawal of the occupation forces. By 1947 the number of strikes was down to eight, and by 1949 to four. But the working class had again demonstrated that it was capable of rapid, effective organisation. Though it lacked the strength and leadership to pose an alternative to the regime, it was clearly the country's most potent force for change.

The national movement

Some members of the bourgeoisie and petit bourgeoisie had profited during the war and private industry had expanded. But many ambitious merchants and capitalists were frustrated by the failure of the imperialist powers to deliver promised aid and to sustain development. By the late 1940s a strong anti-imperialist mood had developed and the bourgeois nationalist Mohammad Mossadeq was able to establish a National Front of parties representing professionals, *bazaaris* and some religious elements.

The Front's main aim was to rid Iran of the British imperial presence in the shape of the Anglo-Iranian Oil Company (APOC had been renamed in 1933). Anglo-Iranian, or AIOC, was viewed as the main channel of imperialist influence and an obstacle to Iranian development. It had continued to suck profits from Iran: between 1945 and 1950 it paid £90 million in royalties to the Iranian government, though its net profits over this period – after deduction of British taxes, royalties and depreciation – were no less than £250 million.[39]

In March 1951 the National Front came to power with Mossadeq as prime minister. It was immediately confronted with a major strike in the oilfields – a response to attempts by AIOC to cut wages and housing subsidies. By April, 45,000 workers were on strike and were met by a government declaration of martial law. After the company reneged on agreements to restore wage levels, the strike was resumed with support from thousands of non-oil workers in Khuzistan and textile workers in other industrial centres – largely the result of activity by the Tudeh. During a series of confrontations the government maintained that action against the company would provoke British military intervention and prejudice the campaign for nationalisation.

When Mossadeq implemented the nationalisation proposals in 1951 Iran was faced by an international oil boycott and a British-led trade boycott. One result was that domestic industry prospered and bourgeois support for the National Front was confirmed. But workers' self-confidence was also growing and a new series of strikes began. The Tudeh, which had led the initial strikes against AIOC, now adopted a position of critical support for the government but could not prevent a wave of disputes. Over two years from mid-1951 there were 158 major industrial disputes.[40] Most began on economic issues but with the revival of the CCFTU there were demands for union rights and, as working-class confidence increased, for political freedoms.

In this atmosphere the government was forced to offer far more than the measures conceded in 1946. Mossadeq limited the Shah's privileges, instituted a purge of the armed forces, signed a decree for land reform and allowed the Tudeh to organise openly.

Each measure further increased workers' confidence and soon there were anti-royalist demonstrations and calls for a republic. Iran was in the grip of a radical mass movement at the heart of which the working class was exercising enormous influence. But as the possibility of revolutionary change became apparent the unstable nature of the National Front was exposed. Bourgeois and petit bourgeois support for the government began to dissolve and, ominously, it became clear that Mossadeq had failed to gain control of the army.

Britain and the US now attempted to use the Shah to dismiss Mossadeq. When the plot was uncovered the Shah fled amid anti-royalist riots in which the Tudeh Party was prominent. But Mossadeq turned against the party, ordering the police and the army to suppress the demonstrations. Intent on exploiting the evident weaknesses of the Front the imperialist governments planned a further coup attempt among monarchist officers. This was accompanied by CIA-organised 'demonstrations' in South Tehran which gave religious leaders the chance to intervene on the Shah's behalf.[41]

The Tudeh refused to mobilise independently, maintaining that only a 'broad alliance' of forces could be effective, and this time the workers' movement – and the government – was doomed. The Shah was soon restored and a campaign of arrests and killings of Tudeh members and worker activists was initiated. Within a year a new deal had been negotiated with the Western oil companies, giving the US oil giants a privileged position.

Bourgeoisie and proletariat in the national movement

The period of the National Front government was a watershed in Iran's modern history. It produced revolutionary possibilities, but resulted in a counter-revolution which wreaked terrible revenge on the opposition in general and the workers' movement in particular. This experience was to mark Iranian society for years to come, having a profound influence on ruling-class strategy and the politics of the left up to the revolution of 1978-79.

On the Iranian left the movement was subsequently seen as an undifferentiated anti-colonial movement, and its failure as a result of the imperialist trade boycott of Iran and the conspiracy which produced the CIA coup.[42] But the events must be seen in a wider context.

The movement reflected the level of development of Iranian capitalism. The bourgeoisie and petit bourgeoisie had been growing in confidence and sought to quicken the pace of modernisation and assume greater control over national resources. They were thus prepared for a limited confrontation with British imperialism, some arguing for the replacement of the Shah, the weakening of the landowners and the establishment of a new *majlis* which would express their own interests.

They had not prepared, however, for the wave of workers' activity which the Mossadeq government had helped to release. They were not willing to see their interests threatened by pressure from below, while they were incapable of standing up to the pressures of imperialism. The bourgeoisie preferred a new deal with Western imperialism – the 1954 oil agreement – to the possibility of the workers' movement gaining strength and the collapse of a system in which they at least enjoyed wealth and privilege. In short, the bourgeoisie and petit bourgeoisie were caught between a rising working class and the demands of imperialism. Once the problem became clear there could be only one outcome – fear of the workers pushed the bourgeoisie towards a new accommodation with the West.

Throughout the National Front's period in power the Tudeh debated the correct strategy to be adopted towards Mossadeq and his government. The party was divided: some members argued that the National Front was a 'progressive' alliance which represented the struggle of the 'national bourgeoisie' against British imperialism and called for further efforts to bring a 'national democratic revolution' to fruition. Others maintained that Mossadeq represented a section of the bourgeoisie which was itself attached to Western interests and that the party should carry on the struggle for change alone.

The argument continued throughout the period of nationalist government, with the tendency critical of Mossadeq always more influential. This was a result of healthy suspicion of governments produced by the party's recent experience of repression – but also of Mossadeq's own early unwillingness to grant reforms and, most important, to the fact that the Tudeh was under enormous pressure from its worker members and the strike movement. Moscow was also critical of Mossadeq, seeing him as too open to Western influence.

However, the Tudeh's reservations about Mossadeq did not lessen its enthusiasm for an alliance with elements of the bourgeoisie and petit bourgeoisie in order to move towards a 'democratic' revolution – one in which the bourgeoisie would play the politically-liberalising role it had played in the West as capitalism was emerging. The Tudeh hoped for a more open *majlis*, freedom of the press and the right to form political parties and trade unions. This view was a consequence of the party's domination by a tradition which stressed the theory of 'stages' – the notion that society must pass through a 'democratic' phase before moving towards socialist revolution. This approach also dictated that the working class should seek an alliance with 'progressive' sections of the capitalist class in a 'popular front' aimed at hastening the move to democratic revolution.

The Tudeh thus sought to align itself with sections of the bourgeoisie, notably the small factory owners. It argued:

There are no fundamental contradictions between the small capitalists and the proletariat. It is true that the former do not work for wages, but they, like the latter, are dominated by the large owners of the means of production. Consequently they are drawn to support the workers against the upper class.[43]

The party adopted a position critical of Mossadeq but on the basis that it would attempt to 'expose' the National Front, mobilising 'progressive' elements of the bourgeoisie on its own account and moving forward towards 'democratic' change.

The strategy was doomed. The Tudeh did not have a place for an insurgent working class within its 'stages' theory and once the implications of the growing strike movement became clear it drew closer to Mossadeq and away from the militants of the factories. The party could not sustain independent action and, unwilling to confront its bourgeois 'partners' in the nationalist alliance, it squandered the opportunity to extend workers' activity and fatally weakened the movement.

The unity the Tudeh sought with 'small capitalists' was an illusion. The bourgeoisie – large and small – soon became fearful of the demands for change expressed by the movement from below and deserted Mossadeq. Real change was only possible on the basis of independent action by the workers' movement – a perspective alien to the tradition the Tudeh had inherited. On the eve of the 1953 coup which restored the Shah, the party urged Mossadeq to join in an alliance of 'progressive forces' against the army and the imperialists. When he refused, the Tudeh stood aside, maintaining that if no 'broad alliance' was possible, resistance to the royalist forces was useless. It decided that the organisation should go underground and wait for more favourable circumstances. It was a suicidal decision – but one the party's strategy had made inevitable.

The permanent revolution

By the time Mossadeq entered government in 1951 the working class had experienced ten years of almost continuous struggle. As early as 1944, after two years of strikes and occupations, the British ambassador in Tehran had commented:

> In Persia we are clearly at the beginning of a new era and are seeing the rise of a new social movement. The advantages which the workers have won are considerable and they will certainly continue to make the employers feel their newly-discovered power.[44]

With the National Front in government and workers enjoying a growing sense of power the movement had developed a dynamic which caused bourgeois leaders to fear cataclysmic upheaval. A senator proclaimed:

> ...foreign-paid agitators are misleading our workers. Every time they exact concessions, they demand more. The result is demonstrations, street battles, strikes and more strikes. They will not be satisfied until production comes to a halt and the country is dragged into an atheistic revolution.[45]

The determination of the most militant sections of workers contrasted sharply with the vacillation and weakness of the bourgeoisie and petit bourgeoisie. Despite bourgeois leaders' radical rhetoric they were incapable of securing even 'democratic' change; they were an obstacle, not an ally for the working class.

Such a situation was not new – it was characteristic of a backward society being penetrated by capitalism. Fifty years earlier Leon Trotsky had anticipated just such a pattern of events when he argued that a process of 'permanent revolution' was necessary to secure change in such a society. The term was first used by Marx and Engels to describe the process by which classes are drawn into political movements which threaten the status quo.[46] It took on new significance after Trotsky's analysis of revolutionary prospects in Russia.

Trotsky argued that in a backward country in which the penetration of capital was expressed by an 'uneven' pattern of development, only the working class could confront the combined weight of imperialism and the domestic bourgeoisie. He maintained that the working class was far stronger, proportionately, than the bourgeoisie which, while it sought political independence, feared the working class more than Russia's tsar and imperialism. While the peasantry might be far larger than the working class, its fragmented and conservative character meant that it could not play an independent role.

Trotsky concluded, therefore, that the working class should not hold back in anticipation of a 'bourgeois' revolution which might secure 'democratic' freedoms. Neither should it trim its demands in fear that 'progressive' bourgeois forces would fall back to a counter-revolutionary position; this, Trotsky argued, they would do anyway. 'The democratic revolution,' he maintained, 'grows over immediately into the socialist, and thereby becomes a *permanent* revolution.'[47]

In the 1905 revolution in Russia the bourgeoisie was, indeed, too weak to confront the tsar, while the working class produced mass strikes and the first *soviets*, or workers' councils, which offered a real threat to the old system. In the revolution of 1917 the bourgeoisie again proved weak and vacillating, while the *soviets* provided the basis for an assault on power by the working class and the establishment of the first workers' state.

The events of 1951-53 in Iran did not produce workers' organisation at the level of the Russian revolutions of 1905 and 1917 – strikes were on a less massive and co-ordinated scale and there were no *soviets*. Nevertheless, workers' activity was at an extremely high level and produced the rapid rise in confidence and demands for change characteristic of periods of mass struggle. The regime certainly believed that radical change was imminent, fearing that 'every time they exact concessions, they demand more'. Meanwhile, as the crisis deepened, the bourgeoisie retreated.

The Tudeh exercised enormous influence within the workers' movement but, as the product of a tradition which wholly rejected Trotsky's analysis, it was destined to play a negative role. It pursued the 'progressive' bourgeoisie relentlessly, only to see it retreat when pressure from below became too great. As in Russia, and on numerous subsequent occasions, all sections of the bourgeoisie had acted to defend their existing class interests. Small capitalists behaved much as the big bourgeoisie. The Tudeh's efforts to form a 'popular front' with sections of the capitalist class failed and the party was savaged by the old regime.

Unable to direct its efforts towards the building of independent workers' organisation and threatening the regime from below, the Tudeh was doomed and the process of permanent revolution terminated. The system survived, though from 1953 one principle was clear – the capacity of the working class to threaten Iranian capitalism was not in doubt. What was in question was the character of its political leadership.

The consolidation of capitalism

The rescue of Iranian capitalism allowed the Shah to embark on a new programme of development. He immediately received aid from the US, and, following the 1954 agreement, much increased oil revenues – between 1954-55 and 1956-57 revenues leapt from $34 million to $181 million.[48] Meanwhile a policy of intense repression reduced working-class activity dramatically: between 1955 and 1957 there were only three major strikes.[49] The bourgeoisie, disciplined by the Mossadeq disaster, was compliant.

But the Shah still needed the support of the bourgeoisie and, like his father, adopted a policy which reflected its economic concerns. He was careful not to antagonise the *bazaar* and began to encourage industrial capital with long-term loans, tax holidays and an offer to privatise state-owned factories. These measures helped produce a surge in industrial activity – between 1957 and 1960 the number of all manufacturing enterprises rose from 45,000 to 70,000 and manufacturing output increased at 20 per cent a year.[50]

The expansion of the system allowed the Shah to consolidate his social base. He integrated the landowners with sections of the merchant class, the bourgeoisie and the petit bourgeoisie into new loyalist political parties – the first attempt by the Pahlavi dynasty to give Iranian capital representation in the political system. But when economic growth faltered in the late 1950s the system proved too rigid to contain renewed dissent. A rapid rise in prices produced popular opposition and an increase in the number of strikes to 20 between 1957 and 1961.[51] Alarmed by the threat of renewed upheaval the US insisted on further economic and political reform.

The Shah conceded a modest land reform and some constitutional changes but by the early 1960s unrest was becoming general and in June 1963 mass demonstrations in almost every major city were put down by the army. The character of the protests was sharply different to those of the 1940s and 1950s. Demonstrations involved many petit-bourgeois elements and religious students and leaders – including Ayatollah Khomeini. But the strike movement was limited to individual workplaces and no new forms of working-class organisation emerged.

Under these circumstances the regime was able to shoot its opponents off the streets. The left was effectively absent. Its almost complete ineffectiveness was an indication of the intensity of the regime's repression, but also of the bankruptcy of the Tudeh, which had all but ceased to function as an opposition, Moscow having determined that the Iranian left should not hinder its attempt to reach an accommodation with the Shah.

The 1963 events hastened the 'White Revolution of the Shah and the People' – a package of measures which included further land reform and limited nationalisation, profit-sharing and welfare provisions. This was a further attempt to widen the base of the regime and had someee important consequences. It broke the stranglehold of the large landowners in certain areas, without affecting the power of the wealthiest families. It also created a larger middle peasantry and helped to introduce 'agri-business' to the countryside; it drove large numbers of poor peasants to the cities where they became available for integration into the industrial sector; and it drew large numbers into the much-expanded state apparatus, helping to create a new petit-bourgeoisie of professionals and administrators.

The Great Boom

The economic growth of the mid-1950s was resumed. Oil revenues again increased dramatically – by 1965 they were $522 million and by 1969 $938 million.[52] Huge sums were spent on the state apparatus but two development plans covering the period 1962-73 also put $10 billion into expanding the infrastructure and boosting manufacturing industry.

Foreign capital now began to take an interest in Iran, attracted by the prospect of sharing in the oil-fed boom which was sweeping the whole Gulf region. Since 1955 the Centre for the Attraction and Promotion of Foreign Investment (CAPFI) had offered favourable terms for foreign capital, including the right to repatriate profits. But there were limitations, including the stipulation that all foreign enterprises should share ownership with Iranian partners. These restrictions, together with the country's reputation for instability, had produced a cautious attitude in the West. It was not until the more favourable conditions of the mid-1960s that foreign capital was attracted by the increasing size of the Iranian market.

By 1969, 90 foreign companies had invested in Iran, half of them from the US,[53] though the foreign sector did not overshadow domestic capital. The state was still the main agent of industrial growth, being responsible for 40-50 per cent of investment. However, the regime also established a set of banks and funds to stimulate private investment, with the result that Iranian capital, which alone was too weak to undertake the investment needed for the establishment of heavy industry and the larger manufacturing enterprises, was steadily extended. During this period landowners who had been dispossessed under land reform, state employees and *bazaaris* moved into the ranks of the bourgeoisie.

The industrial workforce increased dramatically. By 1966 the International Labour Organisation recorded 1.4 million workers in oil, mining and manufacturing and 750,000 in construction and transport. By 1972 these figures had increased to 1.9 million and 965,000 respectively.[54] Wages rose steadily and the regime boasted of growth accompanied by industrial peace.

Boom and bust

Expansion was given a final boost by the oil price rises of 1973. Iran had joined the Organisation of Petroleum Exporting Countries (OPEC) in 1960 and the Shah was an enthusiastic supporter of moves to control production, whatever embarrassment this might cause his Western allies. By December 1973 prices had been pushed up to $11.65 a barrel, from the 1971 price of $1.79. Iran's revenues rose accordingly – from $938 million in 1969 to no less than $22 *billion* in 1974.[55]

A country already involved in a process of rapid development was now awash with capital – but just when the Shah's regime was most loudly trumpeting its success the system moved into a period of instability from which it never recovered.

The Shah had greeted the increase in revenues with a declaration that Iran would become a first-rank world power within a decade. The fifth five-year plan was boosted to a monstrous $69 billion and development programmes, which by

1973 were already producing 30 per cent national growth, were re-drafted to allow for further industrialisation. Inevitably, a massive increase in the state apparatus was planned.

The whole strategy was soon in trouble. Bottlenecks developed in a system in which the infrastructure was unable to cope with huge volumes of imports, while there were serious power failures and general dislocation of industry. At first skilled wages rose rapidly but this encouraged a flood of peasants into the cities and helped precipitate a slump in agricultural production and a steep rise in food prices. Over two years rents in Tehran rose by up to 300 per cent. A few made fortunes in property speculation, importing and commission-dealing, but unskilled workers, the urban poor, the petit bourgeoisie and the peasantry all began to suffer.[56]

Confidence had been growing among workers since the early 1970s and had been boosted by the superboom of 1973-74. In 1971 a dispute at the Shah Jahit textile mill at Karaj, near Tehran, produced fighting which resulted in 13 deaths; in 1973 there was a strike of oil workers; in 1974 a dispute involving 800 workers at Mashin Sazi in Tabriz and a strike of Tabriz transport workers; in 1975 there were 30 strikes including the occupation of the Shahi textile factory near Tehran, which produced a confrontation between workers, students and police.[57]

The changed climate reflected growing confidence among skilled workers, who found themselves in a strong position, mounting short effective strikes for higher pay and improved conditions and often moving jobs regularly, carrying the experience of successful organisation. The leading business journal **Tehran Economist** complained:

> ... wages and salaries are increasing constantly and yet manpower productivity is being neglected ... the individual who used to live on bread and cheese does not find anything less than *chelokebab* [kebab and rice] satisfactory and an unskilled construction worker expects to go to work in a Peykan [car].[58]

The unskilled fared far less well, suffering from the effects of inflation and rocketing rents but being largely unable to protect themselves at work, where their bargaining position was much weaker. In addition, throughout the 1970s rural migration kept great pressure on unskilled wages: between 1956 and 1971 three million peasants moved to the cities, while by the mid-1970s an average of 380,000 migrated each year.[59] One result was that unskilled incomes were a third those of skilled workers, while city slums grew massively, especially in Tehran.

Shaken by the economic downturn, the Shah decided to halt the development programme. Projects were cut and limits set to the expansion of the armed forces and the administration. The scale of the retreat was indicated by the sharp fall in exports. Between 1974 and 1976 they had increased at an annual average rate of 60 per cent. By 1977 the rate was down to 3 per cent.[60]

Demand for labour fell, immediately putting workers and the urban poor under greater pressure and affecting some sections of the petit bourgeoisie. There were further strikes and for the first time in many years a wave of discontent spread through the *bazaar*. The creation of banks and state finance institutions, the progress of industrialisation and the impact of modern methods of distribution had weakened the hold of the *bazaar* on economic life, but it maintained control over two-thirds of the country's retail trade and much of the money-lending vital to small businessmen and artisans. [61] The regime's new turn, with its budget cuts and credit squeeze, produced a crisis for the *bazaar* and many small traders failed.

The regime then turned the screw. Conscious of the need to find a scapegoat for spiralling inflation and rising unemployment, the Shah launched a campaign against corruption, blaming '*bazaar* profiteers' and setting special squads on traders and shopkeepers. Ten thousand 'inspectors' scrutinised shopkeepers' accounts, while special courts jailed 8000 businessmen, shopkeepers and peddlers, exiled 23,000 from their home towns and fined up to 200,000 more.[62] This antagonised not only *bazaaris* but those sections of the bourgeoisie connected to the trading and finance sector.

By 1977 the Shah had succeeded in alienating almost every section of society. Within months the country was on the road to revolution.

Iranian capitalism on the eve of the revolution

All revolutions are shaped by the character of the society in which they are generated. What then was the precise character of Iranian capitalism on the eve of the upheaval?

Iran was still a backward society. Half the population lived in the countryside, where agricultural methods were still primitive. In the cities modern industry was limited to a few sectors and small-scale production was still widespread. But 70 years of development had profoundly changed the country – capital had penetrated Iran and left its mark on the whole of society.

The explanation for the changes lay largely in the role allocated to Iran by the imperialist states. Since the First World War the country had been viewed as an energy source for Western capitalism and the West had made every effort to maintain its influence. In this sense Iran occupied an entirely subordinate position in the international system, one in which the rapid and complete industrialisation characteristic of the core countries of capitalism was out of the question. But this did not mean that development could not take place, rather that it did so on a limited and uneven basis.

The countryside had undergone some changes since the land reform of the 1960s and the majority of families owned some land, though not enough to make an adequate living. Cash-cropping had been replacing subsistence in many parts of the country and in some areas 'agribusiness' had taken over, with huge areas cultivated for wheat and the local population used as a seasonal workforce. A new class of small and medium landowning peasants had emerged and the power of some great landowning families had been reduced. But huge areas still belonged to absentee owners and millions of peasants still barely scratched a living from the soil. While migration had reduced the rural population – by the late 1970s only a third of the Iranian workforce was on the land – the fundamental structures of rural society had not changed.

In the cities change had been far more extensive. The consolidation of capitalism had emphasised the development of what Marx called 'the two great hostile camps' – the bourgeoisie and the proletariat.

Despite the fact that Western capitalism had maintained control over the oil industry a domestic bourgeoisie had been growing steadily. It needed the support of the state and was still small and weak compared to the capitalist classes of rapidly-industrialising countries outside the core of the world system such as India or Brazil. But it had grown from the embryonic formation which at the turn of the century controlled a handful of factories into a well-defined social layer which operated major enterprises.

Its economic weight was expressed by the regime's plans for development in the 1970s. Under the 1973-78 plan the state was to invest $46.2 billion in industry, the private sector was to invest $23.4 billion and foreign capital was to invest $2.8 billion.[63] Even allowing for the errors in the figures produced by the regime – they often bore little relation to the real allocation of resources – the Iranian bourgeoisie was by this time clearly capable of mobilising significant capital on its own account.

The class was highly concentrated. According to a calculation made in 1974, 45 families controlled 85 per cent of the largest companies.[64] But the booms of the 1960s and 1970s had drawn in many new elements from the landowning class, the *bazaar* and the upper levels of the state apparatus, in which there were many officials eager to invest the proceeds of corruption, something rife in the Pahlavi system. The bourgeoisie had also developed an identity which had already been partly expressed in a series of political parties. In the 1940s it backed the National Front, hopeful of replacing the autocracy; later the Shah had some success in integrating loyalist businessmen into official parties operating under the regime's mock-parliamentary system.

The working class had grown quickly. In the 1940s wage-earners constituted 16 per cent of the national labour force – by the mid-1970s the figure had reached 34 per cent. The historian Ervand Abrahamian has commented:

> Reza Shah had brought the modern working class into existence; Muhammad Shah had nourished it to become the single largest class in contemporary Iran.[65]

A precise definition of what constituted the Iranian working class in the late 1970s is complicated by unreliable statistics and the uncertain boundaries between artisan labour and large-scale production. Using 'educated guesses' Abrahamian calculates that there was a core of 880,000 workers in modern industry. This total included more than 30,000 oil workers, 20,000 electrical, gas and power workers, 30,000 fishery and timber workers, 50,000 miners, 150,000 railway workers, dockers and truck drivers, and 600,000 workers in manufacturing plants with more than 10 employees.[66] These are probably conservative estimates.

The total was increased by 392,000 wage-earners employed by urban services and small manufacturing plants, 100,000 in small workshops, 140,000 shop assistants, and 152,000 bank and office workers. The addition of occasional workers among the urban poor – employed in construction and in the smaller factories – and of rural wage-earners, gives a total of 3.5 million. Given the speed with which the economy was expanding by the mid-1970s this is probably also a conservative figure.

The concentration of workers into large units was a feature of the period of expansion which started in the mid-1960s. In 1953 there were 19 factories with more than 500 workers, 300 with between 50 and 500 workers, and approximately a thousand factories with between ten and 49 workers. By 1977 there were 159 factories with over 500 workers, 830 with between 50 and 500, and more than 7,000 with between ten and 49.[67] By international standards the number in large workplaces was not high; nevertheless on Abrahamian's figures this amounted to 20 per cent of the industrial workforce – a dramatic change from the situation a generation earlier.

The regime had ensured that there was no independent workers' organisation through formal workplace groups or unions. Government-controlled unions were no more than extensions of the ubiquitous secret police, *Savak*. Nevertheless, as confidence slowly increased, especially among skilled and semi-skilled workers, networks of activists emerged in many factories. Assef Bayat, who carried out extensive research of factory organisation during the 1978-79 revolution, concluded that large numbers of workers were organised on an informal 'underground' basis and employers faced 'secret cells, which had spontaneously blossomed over the years'.[68] Piecemeal organisation was reappearing – a fact reflected in the increased number of strikes between 1973 and 1979.

Capitalist development meant that the intermediate class – the petit bourgeoisie – had been squeezed. Its traditional status had been under threat for more than 50 years, though the special character of the *bazaar*, with its central role in trade and finance, gave the traditional petit bourgeoisie far more security than in most comparable countries. An ambitious new petit bourgeoisie had emerged, especially in the 1960s – a product of the regime's massive investment in the armed forces and the state administration. Senior officers in the forces, administrators and professionals formed an important new social layer which, until the revolution, was loyal to the regime. In addition, a layer of educated, lower-level professionals and technicians had emerged as a result of the expansion of secondary and higher education.

The process which had produced these changes had created a society in which economic and political contradictions were more evident than ever. The most advanced economic and social forms were found alongside the most simple: in the shadow of petro-chemical plants there were villages without electricity; close to new factories artisans used methods scarcely changed for centuries; in the cities the élite lived like its counterpart in the West, while the mushrooming shanty-towns were scenes of terrible poverty.

Dominating the whole explosive situation was a set of political contradictions which had been deepening ever since Reza Shah set out on the path of national economic development. Notwithstanding their close links with the West, the Pahlavis had been determined to produce an independent modern economy and had helped stimulate the growth of a domestic bourgeoisie and a working class which was of increasing size and political weight. Yet the Shahs operated through an autocracy characteristic of pre-capitalist society. In the early 1950s this had produced a period of conflict in which the bourgeoisie and the working class had played the leading roles in the opposition movement and had themselves engaged in a struggle for power. Twenty-five years later the contradictions had grown more massive: the Shah was no less autocratic, while the two major contending classes were stronger and even more irreconcilably opposed.

2: Revolution

ALMOST EVERY ACCOUNT of the revolution asserts that the first
sections of society to pressure the regime effectively were thee
intellectuals and the religious establishment.[1] This is not the case.
Civil rights protests from writers and lawyers had been mounting
since early 1977, encouraged by US President Carter's pressure on
the Shah for liberalisation. This gave bourgeois leaders the
opportunity to call for reforms and by June 1977 the National
Front felt confident enough to demand that the Shah re-establish
the rights granted by the 1905 Constitutional Revolution – that he
reinstate bourgeois freedoms. But for the regime these demands
were little different from those made by liberal oppositionists over
many years. Not until confronted by mass opposition did the
regime come under real pressure.

In June 1977 the first acts of open defiance were mounted by
the poor of South Tehran. When police were sent in to remove
shanty housing which the Shah felt to be an eyesore in his
'imperial capital' they met unexpected opposition. For weeks
thousands struggled with the police until on 27 August a demonstration of 50,000 slum dwellers drove officials and their bulldoz-
ers from the area, forcing the regime to abandon its plans. This
was the first successful mass protest since the early 1950s and was
an enormous boost to all those opposed to the Shah.[2]

The Tehran events were particularly important for worker
activists who were becoming more open in the organisation of
workplace resistance. As the regime's austerity measures took

effect, and employers cut wages, opposition began to mount in the factories. The number of strikes increased and there were reports of sabotage from all round the country. In July the General Motors plant in Tehran – one of the largest workplaces in the country – was set on fire by workers and according to one estimate, over the next three months there were 130 similar incidents.[3]

By October 1977 there was a new current of confidence running through workplaces and working-class communities. This was a result of growing opposition to the excesses of Iranian capitalism, a reaction to an economic and political crisis that was deepening by the day. While mass working-class opposition to the regime was not to emerge for almost a year, the stirrings of protest were already evident and there were hints of the direction the later upheaval was to take. The stimulus for mass opposition to the Pahlavis was becoming evident; it was the crisis of the Iranian system that was producing a mood of defiance among workers and the poor - not a call to arms from intellectuals or religious figures.

In November 1977, writers, lawyers and academics began a series of public poetry readings which became a focus of liberal opposition. Following police attacks on the meetings and on students at Tehran University, the opposition began to take on a sharper edge. Then, in December, the clergy entered the scene.

Religious opposition to the Pahlavis had long been organised around the Ayatollah Khomeini, who since his exile in 1964 had been living in Iraq. He had gained widespread respect for his sheer staying power, having made his first criticisms of the Pahlavis in the early 1940s though for lengthy periods he had also accommodated to the regime. Exile had hardened his views and for more than ten years a clandestine network of mullahs and seminary students had distributed pamphlets and cassettes of speeches in which he declared monarchy alien to Islam and called for resistance to the regime. Operating through mosques and religious institutions, the Khomeini network had become an important pole of attraction among those who opposed the Shah, though it lacked the capacity to threaten the regime directly.

In December 1977, Khomeini again called for the overthrow of the Shah and the re-establishment of the 1905 constitution. Affected by the heightened atmosphere of dissent, the regime's press responded furiously, attacking Khomeini personally and provoking demonstrations among students and mullahs in the holy city of Qom. Scores of protesters were killed by police and there began a cycle of 40-day mourning ceremonies which allowed the mullahs to place themselves at the head of a movement of seminary students, *bazaaris* and some sections of the urban poor.

Khomeini, still in exile, was surprised by the scale of the protests, but showing characteristic opportunism he moved quickly to try to direct it. He feared a repetition of the 1963 events when, despite his own involvement and that of many leading religious figures, the regime had been able to smash the opposition. He warned: 'If this fire in the hearts of the people is extinguished, it cannot be lit again.' He called for larger demonstrations, the issuing of leaflets and the use of mourning days to 'arouse the population and expose the crimes of the regime'.[4]

Khomeini's supporters spread the protests, using the network provided by the mosques, the seminaries and the *bazaar*, an institution that was to be a key element in the movement. While sections of the landowning class and even the modern bourgeoisie were linked to the mullahs, the *bazaar* had long had a special tie with the mosque. This was an expression of the social origins of Islam, essentially a 'mercantile' ideology.[5] In Iran mosques were physically integrated into the market areas, and merchants, artisans and shopkeepers were among the most devout Muslims and the most prominent backers of the religious establishment.

This relationship had its expression in wider politics, for in the absence of a strong secular alternative – as in 1963 – the mosque had articulated petit-bourgeois discontent. By the late 1970s it was performing a similar role. The *bazaar* was already under economic pressure when, in 1977, the Shah went on to the offensive against small businessmen, sending teams into the *bazaars* to investigate 'corruption'. Hostility to the regime grew rapidly and traders and artisans expressed their discontent through traditional religious channels. This brought much increased numbers on the protest demonstrations and brought Khomeini financial backing – but still the religious network could not mobilise forces of sufficient political weight to shake the regime, for as in 1963 it lacked political muscle.

Throughout the early months of 1978 demonstrations called

by the mullahs and dominated by religious slogans were the focus of protest. Then, in the summer, the strikes resumed, stimulated by a further economic downturn. For a year the government had been obsessed by the need to 'cool' the economy. It now boasted that during this period it had cut industrial expansion by half and reduced growth in construction from an annual rate of 32 per cent to 7 per cent. Wages fell rapidly – from $10 a day for unskilled workers to less than $7 a day, while pressure on skilled workers increased.[6]

By June 1978 disputes were spreading across the country. Most were defensive – workers were attempting to defend wages and conditions – but there were also new, offensive demands. While in Tehran and the south there were strikes over the cancellation of bonuses, in Abadan 600 sanitation workers struck for a 20 per cent wage increase, bonuses and a health scheme. In Behshahr textile workers demanded wage increases and, significantly, free union elections.[7] For the first time since the defeat of 1953 the issue of independent working-class organisation was on the agenda.

The character of demonstrations called by the mullahs began to change. They now drew in the urban poor and, for the first time, a small number of workers. The connection between the economic crisis and the opposition movement was becoming clear to even the most superficial bourgeois commentators. The **Washington Post** observed:

> The recent widespread waves of rioting across Iran are the work of little people lashing out against inflation, unequal distribution of wealth and corruption in high places. 'A year ago you wouldn't have found all these people to go rioting,' a veteran economic analyst said. 'They would all have been working in the construction boom.'[8]

Working class reaction was expressed mainly by the growing strike movement, but for the urban poor there was no such channel of protest. Denied the possibility of collective organisation through the workplace, the *lumpenproletariat* (as Marx had described them) swung behind the mullahs. For some years the influence of the mosque had been growing in the city slums; although there was no institutional relationship – like that between the *bazaar* and the mosque – the poor were drawn to religion as a point of reference in a harsh and disorienting environment. Observing the impact of religious ideas in the fast-changing cities of nineteenth-century Europe, Karl Marx had written: 'Religion is the sigh of the oppressed creature, the heart of a heartless world and the soul of ssoulless conditions. It is the opium of the people.'[9]

Iran's urban poor, washed up on the margins of a crisis-ridden society, also sought meaning in a soulless world. Their struggle against the police and army in the summer of 1977 was an index of their determination to survive; as the Khomeini movement gathered momentum, proving itself the focus of opposition to the regime, the poor discovered the one channel of opposition which seemed to express their anger and their aspirations. As the mullahs combined an appeal for struggle against tyranny with an effort to cleanse Iranian society in the name of Islam, the poor responded in huge numbers.

By August 1978 the scale of protests was worrying the regime's allies. The US called for concessions and the Shah responded by sacking two prime ministers and installing a third, Sharif Emami, whom he believed acceptable to religious leaders. But strikes, sabotage and protest demonstrations continued and the Shah turned to the approach which in the past had served him well. Declaring martial law, he threw down a challenge to the opposition when troops killed thousands of demonstrators in Tehran on 'Black Friday', 8 September.

This show of force aimed, as in 1963, to dissipate the threat to the regime by shooting its opponents off the streets. Had the protest movement remained one dominated by the demonstrations of the mullahs, *bazaaris* and poor, the tactic would probably have worked. But the labour disputes which had been spreading throughout the country now took on a new form: the working class entered the struggle to wield a political weapon that Khomeini could not command: the mass strike.

The workers' movement

On 9 September, 700 workers at the Tehran oil refinery struck against the imposition of martial law and the previous day's massacre. Within 48 hours the strike had spread to refineries at Isfahan, Abadan, Tabriz and Shiraz. On 12 September government censors who had been sent to two Tehran newspapers were greeted by a walkout of all 4,000 employees and Sharif Emami was forced to lift a useless censorship law.[10] On 13 September cement workers in Tehran struck demanding higher wages, freedom for political prisoners and the ending of martial law.[11] On 22 September oil workers in Ahwaz struck and ten days later were joined by 10,000 workers in other areas of the Khuzistan oilfield.[12]

The strikes spread at lightning speed – by early October 50 major plants were closed. These included factories in all the main industrial areas and even remote workplaces such as the copper mines near the southern city of Kerman. Service industries and office workers joined in, with bus drivers, postal workers, hospital staff, teachers, bank employees and hotel workers participating. The demmands now covered a wide range of issues, but centred on wage increases of up to 100 per cent, sacking of management, improved welfare provision, the ending of martial law, the dissolution of *Savak* and the freeing of political prisoners.

The message that the regime might now be facing impossible odds was getting through to many members of the bourgeoisie and top state functionaries. Money left the country at a rate of $50 million a day and bank employees were able to show that a group of the wealthiest individuals, including the prime minister and senior officers of the armed forces, had sent more than $2 billion abroad. The news incensed the mass of the population, giving the strikes and demonstrations a heightened atmosphere and creating an angry mood in the army, where 50 per cent of the rank and file were conscripts who were beginning to identify with the opposition.

The Shah was starting to panic. He vacillated wildly, first persuading the Iraqi regime to expel Khomeini, who moved to France, then offering concessions, including the dissolution of the loyalist Rastakhiz party, amnesties for some prisoners and the arrest of corrupt officials. This only raised confidence in the workers' movement and stimulated wider action. As described by Abrahamian:

By the third week of October, a rapid succession of strikes crippled almost all the *bazaars*, universities, high schools, oil installations, banks, government ministries, post offices, railways, newspapers, customs and port facilities, internal air flights, radio and television stations, state-run hospitals, paper and tobacco plants, textile mills and other large factories.[13]

Some strikes started with demands for wage rises, others with calls for political reform, but before long almost every workplace was demanding both that employers satisfy their immediate demands and that the regime make concessions. The strikes paralysed workplaces for weeks at a time, a resumption of work often leading to the formulation of new demands and further stoppages. At the heart of the action was a highly-organised oilworkers' strike, which, lasting 33 days, paralysed the economy. The country was in turmoil: the regime and the mass movement were locked in a life-or-death struggle.

Liberal bourgeois politicians tried to mediate between the Shah and the religious leadership, which was the only formal representative of any part of the mass movement. Bazargan and Sanjabi of the National Front travelled to Paris to meet Khomeini and arrange his reconciliation with the regime. They failed – Khomeini had grasped the significance of the opportunity presented to him and was unwilling to concede his own increasingly prominent position.

Bazargan insisted that he did not want a revolution. He told Khomeini, 'The people are not ready to cope with freedom.' The Ayatollah insisted: 'No gradualism, no waiting. We must not lose a day, not a minute. The people demand an immediate revolution.'[14] Khomeini was now riding the wave of struggle, endorsing strikes and the street clashes which were taking place daily, while he called for further action. He had become the only nationally-accepted leader in the movement.

In early December the oil workers began a further total strike, causing the government losses of $74 million a day in revenue. Troops were sent to the oilfields, but in vain. *Bazaaris* joined the protests – the Tehran *bazaarr* closing for a week – while the first cracks appeared in the armed forces as some troops refused to fire on demonstrators and mutinies occurred in several large barracks.

The Shah now tried a new combination of carrot-and-stick, appearing on television to admit past errors, announce the arrest of leading figures and concede government employees' wage demands. Meanwhile he tried unsuccessfully to crush the strikes. Demonstrations reached huge proportions; on 11 December two million protesters marched in Tehran under the slogans 'Hang the American puppet', 'Arms for the people' and 'The Shah must go'. Soldiers began to desert – the state machine was crumbling.

The Shah made one last attempt to hang on, appointing Shahpur Bakhtiar of the National Front as prime minister. But now even his key supporters, the Americans, were prepared to desert him. It was clear to Washington that the Shah could no longer guarantee Western oil supplies. His presence would continue to deepen opposition activity and might even stimulate similar action against US allies in the Arab Gulf states. The Carter administration decided it would be better off without him.

On 16 January 1979, with the country still in the grip of strikes and demonstrations, the Shah left for Egypt.

The insurrection

The state was now disintegrating. When Khomeini returned on 1 February 1979 he was met by officers who pledged the support of key units of the armed forces. Round the country desertions were occurring daily and when Bakhtiar used the army police and the Imperial Guard against a mutiny of *homafars* – air force cadets – fighting erupted.

The cadets were joined by members of the opposition guerrilla organisations, the Fedayeen and Mojahidin, hitherto largely bystanders in the revolutionary events. With their support the cadets secured their own base and distributed weapons to oppositionists across Tehran. Over a period of 24 hours the insurgents destroyed much of the Shah's war machine, capturing factories and armouries, military bases, prisons, the television station, the *majlis* and the Tehran military academy. Round the country bases were overrun as the officer corps collapsed. Bakhtiar went underground and Bazargan, whom Khomeini had declared prime minister, took over.

A final effort by remnants of the Shah's forces to mount a coup was snuffed out in two days. By 16 February the Pahlavi state had been broken.

The mass strike

Most accounts of the revolution up to February 1979 view it as an undifferentiated people's struggle against the Pahlavis. It was indeed a mass popular movement – but one in which the decisive role was played by the working class.

Demonstrations were the most visible form of protest. The majority of demonstrators, especially in the first six months of 1978, were connected with the mosque and the *bazaar*. But these sections of the population did not initiate the key periods of struggle, nor were they capable of sustaining the activity which led to the Shah's fall.

At two vital points – in July and September 1978 – it was workers' action, independent of other elements of the opposition, which placed the regime under threat. Not until the strike movement was well under way was the religious leadership able to exert the influence that allowed Khomeini to call for further industrial pressure. Even then the movement was not wholly under the direction of the religious leadership – as we shall see, it had a life of its own.

The character of the 1978 strikes has caused confusion. There has been a widespread assumption that they were divorced from wider political concerns, that they were not part of the formal opposition to the Shah and were thus 'unpolitical'. In fact, most strikes between July and October began on economic issues, while later many started by demanding political change and then produced programmes of economic demands. During the period of mass action political demands were transformed into economic demands, and vice versa.

This was not a new phenomenon. Such a pattern has characterised almost every mass workers' movement. Bourgeois analysts and those who seek change by gradual reform of capitalism assert that there is a strict dividing line between economics and politics. They maintain that struggles to improve economic conditions and those which take up political issues are distinct and separate. By contrast, revolutionary Marxists have maintained that there is no such 'Chinese wall' between the two and that in periods of heightened class struggle economic issues grow into political ones, while political demands stimulate calls for economic struggle.

The Polish revolutionary Rosa Luxemburg, who studied the strikes of the Russian revolution of 1905, pointed out that such mass strikes have a special quality. She argued:

> The movement does not go only in one direction, from an economic to a political struggle, but also in the opposite direction. Every important political mass action, after reaching its peak, results in a series of economic mass strikes. And this rule applies not only to the individual mass strike, but to the revolution as a whole. With the spread, clarification and intensification of the political struggle, not only does the economic struggle not recede, but on the contrary it spreads, and at the same time becomes more organised and intensified. There exists a reciprocal influence between the two struggles. Every fresh attack and victory of the political struggle has a powerful impact on the economic struggle, in that at the same time as it widens the scope for the workers to improve their conditions and strengthens their impulse to do so, it enhances their fighting spirit. After each soaring wave of political action, there remains a fertile sediment from which sprout a thousand economic struggles. And the reverse also applies. The workers' constant struggle constitutes, so to speak, the permanent reservoir of working-class strength from which political struggles always imbibe new health.
>
> In a word, the economic struggle is the factor that advances the movement from one political focal point to another. The political struggle periodically fertilises the ground for the economic struggle. Thus we find that the two elements, the economic and the political, do not separate themselves from one another during the period of the mass strikes in Russia, not to speak of negating themselves, as pedantic schemes would suggest.[15]

All the upheavals that have offered revolutionary possibilities under capitalism have been characterised by such strikes, which have not only paralysed the system but have produced among workers a new awareness of their own power. This can stimulate new forms of working-class organisation – strike committees, and, at a higher level, workers' councils that link striking workplaces. Such was the experience in 1905 and 1917 in Russia, and, in the years following the 1917 revolution, in Germany and Italy. There were similar developments in Spain and France in 1936, Hungary in 1956 and Poland in 1980.

In revolutionary crises the effectiveness of strikes and of the organs of direct democracy they produce varies greatly according to the numbers, degree of unity and political leadership of those involved. At the highest level, as in the Russian revolutions of 1905 and 1917, the mass strike produces new forms of organisation – the workers' council or *soviet* – and great changes in the consciousness of those involved. Divisions between workers in different industries, cities and ethnic groups dissolve; religious ideas become less significant; and the main issue becomes that of the irreconcilable difference between the interests of the ruling class and those of the workers' movement.[16]

Much of the Iranian experience in 1978 conformed to the pattern described by Luxemburg and since seen elsewhere. Mass strikes combined economic and political demands – as Luxemburg put it, 'cause and effect interchanged'. Workers moved from demands for increased wages to a call for free unions; from demanding 'Death to the Shah' to calling for a shorter working week. They also produced new forms of organisation, with workers' committees appearing in many workplaces to organise strike action, their members elected by the workforce. And as the end of the regime came near many capitalists and managers fled, leaving the committees as sole authority in factories and offices.

In some industries the level of organisation was extremely high. The oil workers, the most powerful section of the working class, organised two long strikes during which the demands of production, refinery and staff workers were remarkably similar. On 29 October, during the first, 33-day strike, the staff at Ahwaz formulated an extensive programme of demands which illustrated their own sense of power and the new horizons which were opening up. They demanded:

1. An end to martial law
2. Full solidarity and co-operation with the striking teachers in Ahwaz

3. Unconditional release of political prisoners
4. Iranianisation of the oil industry
5. All communications to be in the Persian language
6. All foreign employees to leave the country [Points 4, 5 and 6 reflected workers' resentment of foreign management and the imperialist traditions of the industry]
7. An end to discrimination against women staff employees and workers
8. The implementation of a law dealing with the housing of oil workers and staff employees
9. Support for the demands of the production workers, including the dissolution of *Savak*
10. Punishment of corrupt high government officials and ministers
11. Reduced manning schedules for offshore drilling crews[17].

The effectiveness of the oil workers' action was reflected in the willingness of Hushang Ansary, head of the National Iranian Oil Company, to meet the committee. Workers' representatives reported that he said he would 'consider the economic demands but that the others were outside his sphere. We told him we were not going to make any distinction between our economic and non-economic demands. We told him we had only one set of demands'.[18]

The oil workers were among the best organised, but the experience of elected committees raising such wide-ranging demands was general. Employers who for years had regarded their workforce with contempt were forced to negotiate or, feeling their position to be hopeless, to flee, leaving their businesses to the workers.

The longer the strikes went on, the more persistent became the demands, with economic demands more elaborate, and political demands – dominated by the assertion that the Shah must go – more general.

Limitations of the mass strike

But in one crucial sense the movement of 1978 differed from that of the most developed mass strikes: it did not produce independent organs of workers' power like the *soviets* of revolutionary Russia.

The *soviet* first appeared during the mass strikes of the Russian revolution of 1905. It began as a strike committee among print workers in St Petersburg but soon grew into a delegate body which represented workers in all areas of the city's industry. It was based on the power of workplace organisation, cutting across divisions between industries and between trade unions. It discussed economic issues but was also intensely political. Its very first declaration called for use of 'the final, powerful weapon of the world workers' movement – the general strike'.[19]

The *soviet* of 1905 was eventually destroyed by the Russian state but in 1917 it again emerged from the strike movement. Within days of the outbreak of mass strikes which were to topple the regime of the Tsar, a St Petersburg *soviet* was established to which workers sent elected delegates to meet in a central body. As before, this discussed economic issues such as wage increases and the length of the working day, together with political questions such as the whole future of the revolutionary movement.

It was within the *soviet* that revolutionary socialists put forward their arguments about the need to destroy the capitalist state and establish a new, socialist order. When the Bolshevik Party was able to win its argument for 'All Power to the *Soviets*', the working class was finally in a position to mount an assault on the old state and take power in its own name. The *soviet* was the organ of workers' power which made the revolution possible. It was an expression of direct workers' democracy – a product of the old system which contained the seeds of a new, classless society.

Such bodies developed in Germany in 1918 and 1919, in Spain in 1936, and in Hungary in 1956. In none were they able to achieve the success of the Russian *soviets* of 1917 – largely because the condition for successful revolution, the existence of a revolutionary workers' party, was not satisfied. Nevertheless, independent workers' councils did emerge, co-ordinating the activity of workplace strike committees and cutting across many divisions within the working class.

Why did the mass strikes in Iran not produce such organisations?

The Iranian strikes were long-lasting – many workplaces were on strike for much of a three-month period from October 1978. Many also produced democratically-elected strike committees. But while the level of organisation within factories, plants and offices was high, there was little or no co-ordination outside the workplaces.

The conditions for such co-ordination certainly existed. As Assef Bayat's study of the strike committees put it: 'The revolutionary crisis had furnished the material basis for such organisations; and their organisational and functional forms were present in embryo.'[20] Indeed, there was limited co-ordination across industries: strike committees at the giant Isfahan steel plant negotiated with railway workers to carry coal to the furnaces; oilworkers met rail workers to discuss the transport of fuel for domestic consumption; and, most important, workers' representatives from the oil industry met to decide on production levels and on priority cases for fuel supply – allocating the country's most precious resource.[21]

But at no point did the movement produce integrated committees or councils on the model of Russia, Germany or Spain – bodies capable of co-ordinated discussion and activity which would allow workers to pose an alternative to Iranian capitalism. The most important reason for their incomplete development was the existence of another pole of attraction within the workers' movement – that of the religious establishment. It was the clergy, with their networks built around the mosque, who exercised the main influence on affairs *outside* the factories.

While the level of the mullahs' involvement in the strike movement varied widely, they were able to gain some influence in most workplaces. This was exercised directly by individual members of the clergy and through the mosques and neighbourhood committees, which often took the lead in street protests. Neighbourhood groups called demonstrations, produced propaganda, arranged transport, distributed food and protected local activists. Meanwhile, though they were at the heart of the movement, the strike committees limited themselves to workplace affairs.

As a result, the weight of the strike committees was not great enough to displace that of the mosque. The development of the committees was arrested; they did not produce *soviets*.

This had implications for the dynamic of the whole movement. The strike committees expressed the aspirations of the most militant workers – they were the centres of debate and activity, sustaining mass action to the point at which the regime was broken. But because they did not generalise working class experience across workplaces and industries they could not be forums in which workers confronted the problem of making strategy for the whole movement.

Bayat expressed the problem precisely:

> While the workers indeed controlled all revolutionary activities within the workplaces, they did not and could not exert their leadership upon the mass movement as a whole. This leadership was with someone else: Khomeini and the leadership associated with him.[22]

The strike committees made the revolution possible: alas, they did not lead it.

But why was the religious establishment able to assert itself in such a way? Why could its influence penetrate the workplaces so extensively? How was it possible for the mosque to exert such power *within* the workers' movement?

The religious opposition

The religious leadership saw the early phases of the revolution as an extension of their own opposition to the regime. The movement, insisted Khomeini, 'was founded by the able hand of the clerics alone, and with the support of the great, Islamic nation. It was and is directed, individually or jointly, by the leadership of the clerical community.' It was, he said 'one hundred per cent Islamic'.[23] But this comment was far from accurate – it was not a description of the movement, but a reflection of Khomeini's ambition for the direction it should take.

Religious leaders had seldom dominated Iran's opposition movements. There was nothing inherently 'radical' about the ideology of Shia Islam or its leaders: the faith produced both quietist and activist currents. Some ayatollahs had supported opposition movements, others had been part of the court at Tehran. Leading religious figures had been prominent in the agitation that preceded the Constitutional Revolution of 1905 – but they played a similar role in the coup that brought the Shah back to power in 1953.

There were also strict limits to the ideas of even the most activist religious leaders – none embraced the aspirations of the mass movements which threatened radical change. Rather, they supported the protest movements that emerged when the bourgeoisie and petit bourgeoisie were challenging the regime for greater freedoms. Indeed, during the two key periods of mass struggle after the First and Second World Wars, religious leaders were prominent largely as opponents of the movement from below – a reflection of the close ties between the *ulama* (religious leaders), the landowners and the *bazaar*. When the masses were absent from the scene – as in the early 1960s – the mullahs exercised far greater influence.

Khomeini took the 'activist' current to its furthest extension, but there was much in his history that expressed the highly conservative nature of the religious establishment. He first attracted attention in the 1920s, when, as a student in the religious centre of Qom, he showed considerable talent and was soon giving lectures on ethics to large audiences. This resulted in his first clash with the authorities: Reza Shah was engaged in reducing all opposition and religious gatherings were regarded as potentially dangerous.

The reform programme Reza Shah pursued throughout the 1920s and 1930s also brought Khomeini into conflict with the regime. The Shah was determined to modernise Iran and set out to eliminate Islam as a cultural force, secularising the law and the educational system – moves that much reduced the influence of the religious establishment. Khomeini witnessed repeated clashes between the regime and the clergy, but chose to play no role in organised opposition.[24]

Khomeini did not express his political views in print until 1941. Then, in **Kashf ol-Asrar** ('The Unveiling of Secrets') he attacked the regime as illegitimate and cruel, attributing the situation to the Shah's rejection of Islamic principles and his offensive on the religious establishment. Khomeini was critical of the Shah's adoption of Western legal codes and in particular of his extension of some freedoms to women.

But still Khomeini was far from rejecting the monarchy or even the Pahlavi autocracy. As Shaul Bakhash has pointed out:

While stressing the desirability of permitting the *ulama* a large measure of supervision over governmental affairs, he did not claim for them the right to rule, or require the *ulama* to refrain from all forms of co-operation with the government. On the contrary, he indicated the readiness of the the *ulama* to accept a far more limited role and to co-operate even with bad governments in upholding the state because 'they consider even this rotten administration better than none at all'.[25]

Khomeini maintained that the religious leadership served as 'a pillar of the state'. It protected the country against foreign, non-Islamic influence; suppressed attempts at insurrection; and ensured internal order. By the same token, Khomeini argued, the government must protect and uphold the religious leadership. Such a two-way relationship was the guarantee of healthy government.[26] Khomeini's opposition to the regime was extremely limited; his deeply conservative ideas were modified only by concern that the Shah should not upset the balance between the religious establishment and the state.

The 1940s and early 1950s produced a highly effective mass movement that confronted the regime and its Western backers – but Khomeini shunned political involvement, despite the establishment of 'fundamentalist' groups with which he was later to claim much in common.[27] He was said to be unwilling to offend the leading religious figure of the period, Ayatollah Burujerdi, often seen at the Pahlavi court. By endorsing such religious leaders, who were linked to the regime and intensely hostile to the aims of the most advanced sections of the working class movement, Khomeini effectively backed the Shah.

Khomeini did not emerge as an independent political figure until the early 1960s. Even then, he was not stimulated by concern for the plight of the masses but by the Shah's introduction, under us pressure, of a package of reforms. When, in 1962, the Shah proposed to give women the vote in local elections, Khomeini was outraged by what he saw as an offence to Islamic principles – 'an attack on our chaste women'.[28] He was also fiercely opposed to a further effort to secularise education and to a land reform which the religious leadership saw as a violation of the sanctity of private property. This threatened *waqf* property –

religious endowments – and the financial independence of mosques, seminaries and the religious establishment as a whole.

Burujerdi was now dead and Khomeini publicly opposed the Shah. He did not see himself as a representative of the oppressed masses, but of the religious establishment, confronting a Shah he characterised as an opponent of Islam. But in the absence of secular opposition – which had become a victim of repression and its own bankrupt politics – Khomeini was a figure around which dissident secular elements could organise, and he found himself a pole of attraction for both religious and secular oppositionists. This, Bakhash remarks, 'gave him a sense of the power the *ulama* could wield in a confrontation with the government ... a lesson Khomeini did not forget.'[29]

In 1963 the regime attacked religious students protesting against the reform policy. Khomeini pronounced the Shah an enemy of Islam and an agent of the West and its ally, Israel. He was arrested and demonstrations took place in five major cities. When the Shah ordered the protests put down, the army took to the streets and 200 demonstrators were killed. Mullahs and seminary students continued to rally around Khomeini and a nervous government decided not to bring him to trial.

Despite the regime's hesitation – its first sign of weakness in ten years – Khomeini backed off. He still regarded the regime as in need of reform, rather than removal. He declared: 'The government should stay. But it should respect the laws of Islam, or at least the constitution'.[30] For several months he adopted a lower profile but in 1964 attacked a new law giving immunity to American forces in Iran. This time there were no demonstrations of support and the Shah was able to banish him to Turkey without difficulty. Shortly afterwards, Khomeini moved to Iraq, where he spent the next 13 years.

Exile hardened Khomeini's opposition to the regime. He began to elaborate a new critique of the monarchy and to appeal to the mass of Iranians to oppose a regime of 'tyranny and unbelief'. For the first time he declared that the monarchy as an institution was alien to Islam and argued for an Islamic state on the model of the Prophet Muhammad's *umma*, or Islamic community, of the seventh century. He also argued that Islamic law must govern such a society and that, as the experts in such law were the clerics themselves, they should govern the future Islamic state.

But these ideas were largely for the consumption of Khomeini's active supporters among the mullahs and seminary students. In his wider appeals, Khomeini was careful to restrict his statements to populist issues. As Abrahamian points out, he was careful not to distance himself from any potential supporters:

> He carefully avoided making public pronouncements, especially written ones, on issues that would alienate segments of the opposition: issues such as land reform, clerical power, and sexual equality. Instead, he hammered the regime on topics that outraged all sectors of the population: the concessions granted to the West, the tacit alliance with Israel, the wasteful expenditure on arms, the decay of agriculture, the rise in the cost of living, the housing shortage and the sprawling slums, the widening gap between rich and poor, the suppression of newspapers and political parties, the creation of a vast bureacratic state, and the gross violations of the constitutional laws.[31]

As a result, by the late 1970s Khomeini was viewed as the most intransigent opposition leader. He supervised a loose network of supporters spread across Iran, based on the mosques and the seminaries. This was far from being a political party: it had no formal ideology, and while owing broad allegiance to Khomeini, was divided by loyalties to other ayatollahs, sects and religious organisations. Nevertheless, in the absence of effective organisation among secular parties the Khomeini network was the only coherent national opposition.

Khomeini and the struggle for leadership

For Khomeini, the mass movement which emerged in 1977 and 1978 was 'founded by the clerics alone'. But the poor of Tehran who battled against the regime in 1977 were not motivated principally by religious belief, or directed by the mullahs; nor, later in the year, were the liberals and intellectuals whose meetings increased the momentum of the protest movement. Only from January 1978 did Khomeini and his supporters exert independent leadership, calling anti-regime demonstrations.

Then, the ability of the religious network to spread the protests through the mosques was of immense importance, but still the base of the movement was limited to the mullahs' traditional constituencies – the *bazaar* and the urban poor – social layers which lacked the weight to challenge the regime.

Only when the strikes of July and August 1978 began did the Shah face a real threat. And these disputes, and the mass strikes which began in September, were not directed by the mullahs. The demands for economic and political change were strikingly similar to those raised in mass working-class movements elsewhere – the strike movement was clearly secular in character. While, by October, many striking workplaces were calling for the return of Khomeini – on the basis that he was the most prominent opposition leader – this was only one of a host of demands of a non-religious character. Far from being 'one hundred per cent Islamic' and 'directed by the clerics', it was driven by the enthusiasm of the rank and file.

Khomeini's solution was to capture the workers' movement. Showing great skill, he trimmed his whole approach to match the radical tone of the masses' demands. He already had the reputation of being an outspoken critic of the regime whom the Shah had been unable to silence. Now he added a radical dimension to the image. While he had long opposed those who attempted to synthesise Islam with radical secular ideologies, he too now spoke of 'revolution'. He attacked capitalism and spoke of the need for a society in which there would be justice and democracy.

He also 'discovered' the power of the strike. In October, with strikes already exploding across the country, he called for solidarity action. In January 1979 he urged greater efforts against the regime: 'the honourable people of Iran ... must continue their strikes', he insisted.[32]

Why was Khomeini able to move so far from the traditional values of the religious establishment? One reason was the flexible approach he had adopted in exile, which had made him champion of all manner of radical causes, even though his intention was to establish a deeply conservative regime under clerical control. But just as important was the fact that his most important social base, the petit bourgeoisie, was being rapidly politicised. Throughout 1978 the Shah increased pressure on the *bazaar*, which he sought to present as a scapegoat for deepening economic crisis. As the petit bourgeoisie sought more radical solutions, the Khomeini network, itself under pressure from the regime, responded by providing a focus for opposition.

As a result, by the time the strike wave began, Khomeini and his supporters had already adopted a position more radical than that taken by any section of the religious establishment in modern Iranian history. Thus Khomeini's accommodation to the workers' movement did not necessitate an entirely new approach – he already expressed the anger of a radicalised petit bourgeoisie and was soon able to make the further rhetorical gestures that allowed an alignment with the militants of the factories.

Khomeini was adept at the art of *taqiyya*, or dissimulation, long recognised in the Shiite tradition as a legitimate device whereby true beliefs could be disguised under adverse circumstances. Ayatollah Motaheri, who was close to Khomeini, has spelt out Khomeini's approach:

> He presented the concepts of class contradictions, freedom and justice using Islamic criteria and the rich background of Islamic culture ... The society received these ideas in good faith.[33]

But while speaking of 'class' and 'freedom', Khomeini was still careful not to specify the character of the changes he really sought. He was frequently asked about his aim for the movement and his vision of a new Iran. He maintained : 'There is a programme ... the programme is Islam and it is better and more progressive than the programme implemented by the colonialists.' When asked if he would give details, the ayatollah insisted, 'Not yet ... We will in the future announce all our political, economic and cultural policies.'[34]

Among his few promises was a categorical denial that the religious leadership would play a central role, or that he would assume a position in a new government. In November 1978 he asserted, 'neither my age, not my desire, nor my religious position permits such a thing'.[35] The clergy would play merely a 'guiding' role, he maintained. 'The people' would be sovereign. It was these pronouncements which set the tone for the adoption by the whole religious establishment of what one writer called its 'remarkable anti-imperialist and anti-oppression rhetoric'.[36]

This approach made Khomeini and his supporters plausible allies of the striking workers, but still it did not mean they exerted direct influence on workplace affairs. It was only because of the absence of a coherent secular alternative that the religious leadership was able to extend its influence further into the working class. And this was a slow process – even after February 1979, with Khomeini in power, Bayat comments that pro-regime workers were 'a tiny stratum'.[37] But as long as the clergy did not antagonise the strike movement, and provided there was no secular alternative rooted in the working class, the religious establishment could increase its influence by default.

It did so by remaining the most intransigent national opposition to the Shah. Despite attempts by bourgeois politicans such as National Front leaders Sanjabi and Bazargan to win Khomeini to a compromise solution, the ayatollah remained adamant: 'The Shah must go.' Such an attitude confirmed the ayatollah's dominance among national opposition figures, especially when his position in exile proved an enormous asset – broadcasts from abroad gave him a huge national audience.

Khomeini had one other advantage – the religious network itself. This had consolidated during 1978, swinging behind Khomeini, and by the time the strike wave broke it had been active for months. Thus while the political weight of the mass movement was exercised through the factories, much of the general political activity was organised through the mosque. This meant that the religious establishment possessed an important advantage over the strikers and their workplace committees. Its network played a central role in organising demonstrations, producing propaganda and protecting activists.

While the mullahs could not mobilise the working class, they could dominate the movement of the streets and, through Khomeini's radical rhetoric, project themelves as the embodiment of the national opposition. As a result the development of the strike committees was arrested. The mosque confined the horizons of the workers' committees, which never extended beyond the workplace.

But why was the religious network the sole national opposition? Why was there no secular opposition capable of asserting the independence of the workers' comittees? The answer must be sought in the failure of all the secular currents, and, most important, in the bankrupt politics of the left.

The failure of the left

Among the most startling aspects of the whole revolutionary experience in Iran was that no secular organisation was able to play a leading role in the mass movement. In the case of the bourgeois National Front, this could be attributed to the fact that its approach was hostile to all manifestations of working class activity. In the case of the left the problem was more complex – the result of a tradition which had distorted all the principles of revolutionary Marxism.

The National Front and the Liberation Movement

After the 1953 coup the National Front had disintegrated but with the relaxation of police suppression in 1960 it re-formed and some members played a role in organising the 1963 uprising. Others, however, adopted mild reformist strategies, helping to contain the mass movement. Following the 1963 events the Front was again banned and for 15 years effectively disappeared as a national political organisation.

The Front had also spawned the Liberation Movement, which included a wide range of figures from liberals to radical 'neo-Marxists' such as Ali Shariati.[38] The Liberation Movement argued that the exiled religious leadership, principally Khomeini, had become the main opposition to the regime. Like the Front, it lacked coherent national organisation and could not intervene effectively in the mass movement, but its supporters were clear where their loyalty lay – they were largely unquestioning supporters of the religious leadership.

During the events of 1977-78 these two currents acted in support of those bourgeois and petit bourgeois elements who resented the Shah but whose main aim was to stabilise Iranian capitalism. They were opponents of the mass movement, backing attempts at compromise launched by figures such as Bazargan and Sanjabi.

The Tudeh

By the 1970s the Tudeh had passed through a generation of inactivity. After the 1953 coup the party subjected itself to a fierce self-criticism, though rather than recognise its failure to lead the mass movement to power, the party criticised itself for pursuing a 'left sectarian' policy and not fully supporting the Mossadeq government. It declared that the main tasks confronting the opposition were now:

> ... the overthrow of the anachronistic monarchy, the destruction of the reactionary state machinery, the abolition of big capitalists and landlords, and the transfer of power from these classes to the classes and strata that are patriotic and democratic – ie the workers, peasants, urban petit bourgeoisie (traders, shopkeepers and craftsmen), patriotic and progressive intelligentsia, and strata of the national bourgeoisie. In short, the task is to establish a national democratic republic.[39]

The party was even more clearly wedded to the policies which had proved such a disaster during the nationalist government.

The Tudeh now passed through a long period during which it lost many former supporters – a result of the regime's renewed crackdown, but also of increasing dissatisfaction with Moscow's desire to draw closer to the Shah and the party's determination to avoid confrontation with the regime. Following defections to a new pro-Chinese organisation established after the Sino-Soviet split, the Tudeh Party became little more than a shadowy network of individuals. A modest recovery in the early 1970s allowed the reconstitution of part of the industrial base but could not repair the damage done over almost 20 years of inactivity.

When the revolutionary storm broke in 1978 the party was ill-equipped to intervene. Reflecting Moscow's uncertainty over the outcome of the crisis, it was slow to identify with the militancy of the movement, later attempting to compensate by uncritical support for Khomeini.

The Fedayeen

While by the late 1970s the National Front and the Tudeh had ceased to offer any effective alternative, the organisations of the 'new left' had some claim to represent the aspirations of the masses who opposed the Shah. Their ideas influenced a whole generation of young activists.

Following the defeat of the early 1950s, two new currents had emerged on the left: one from within the Tudeh Party, the other from the National Front. The founders of the Fedayeen were critics of the Tudeh who had been active in the party's youth organisation. The scale of the 1953 defeat, the passivity of the party in succeeding years, and the conduct of Moscow in successfully seeking an accomodation with the Shah had alienated many young activists. Initially they were vague about their analysis of Iranian society, but by the mid-1960s they were coming under the influence of the theories of 'dependency', national liberation struggle and guerrilla warfare which were sweeping opposition movements worldwide.

Attracted by the apparent success of the guerrilla strategy in Latin America and the Middle East – in particular by the Cuban experience, the victory of the Algerian FLN and the successes of the Palestine Liberation Organisation (PLO) – the Fedayeen's early theorists developed a new approach to Iran. The Jazani-Zarafi group – which fused with the Ahmadzadeh-Pouyan group in 1970 to form the Organisation of Iranian People's Fedai Guerrillas, or Fedayeen – argued that it was necessary to break from the Tudeh policy of 'inactive survival' by initiating armed struggle against the regime. It maintained that such a strategy would stimulate the workers' movement, producing the conditions under which a new socialist party could emerge which would itself take on the regime, 'subjectively' producing the conditions necessary for revolution.

As the group came more completely under the influence of the 'Latin American' school – Castro, Guevara, Debray, Frank and others – this approach was modified. The group put forward a new analysis of Iranian development, arguing that the country was being transformed from a 'feudalistic' to a '*comprador* bourgeois*' system. Under such circumstances it was necessary to launch a liberation struggle which would rid Iran of the local agents of imperialism – the *comprador* bourgeoisie. The chosen method of struggle was 'armed propaganda' which would counter the regime's 'fascist methods' by mobilising forces that the regime's repression had placed in a state of 'confusion'. The armed struggle would also replace the Tudeh's policy of 'wait and see' as 'armed acts' stimulated revolutionary fervour among the masses.

By the late 1960s the Jazani-Zarifi group was arguing that armed struggle was the sole effective strategy for the left in Iran. Its leading theorist, Bizan Jazani, wrote:

> We have no doubt about the fact that any political confrontation with the system that basically rests its power on military dictatorship is not possible except through armed struggle.[40]

On this basis the group began the organisation of cells and to prepare to launch a guerrilla war, with the emphasis on the countryside.

At this stage the Fedayeen analysis was going through frequent revisions, though its premises remained consistent. An example of the elaboration being offered came from Amir Parviz Pouyan, in **The Necessity of Armed Struggle and The Rejection of the Theory of Survival** and Massoud Ahmadzadeh in **Armed Struggle: Both Strategy and Tactic**, two books written in the late 1960s. Like Jazani, Pouyan argued that the left faced two overwhelming problems: the regime's repression and the apathy of the masses. As a result, he maintained, socialist activity in the working class was impossible. Modifying the ideas of Mao Tse-tung, he argued:

> In a situation where there are no firm links between the revolutionary intelligentsia and the masses, we are not like fish in the water but rather like isolated fish surrounded by threatening crocodiles ... Terror, repression and the absence of democracy have made it impossible for us to create a working class organisation.[41]

What was needed, Pouyan argued, was an armed struggle which would 'jolt' the masses, convincing them that the regime was not immune to the opposition, and which could provide a focus which could group revolutionary elements. Armed struggle, the only alternative to the Tudeh's 'wait and see' policy, would set up a 'dynamic' which would sustain the left.

Amhadzadeh added that it was necessary to reconsider experiences in countries such as Russia and China, where revolutionaries had been able to operate in 'a spontaneous mass movement'. In the Iranian situation, where workers were passive, it was necessary to *create* a movement – and this could only be achieved if a party was ready to intervene and lead the struggle by example. He asked:

> Why should we believe in the dogma that a massive uprising could only be initiated by the masses themselves? Didn't the Cuban Revolution show us that a small guerrilla outfit is capable of initiating a massive uprising and gradually bringing the workers into struggle?[42]

It was with these ideas in mind that in 1971 the Fedayeen launched the Siakal raid. While the organisation's aims were modest – to free a captured guerrilla held in a gendarmerie outpost – the operation was a disaster, all 13 guerrillas being killed or captured. Despite this setback and the regime's success in penetrating many of the organisation's cells and capturing a host of its leading members, guerrilla activity in the countryside remained the Fedayeen's main strategy for the next seven years.

Between 1971 and 1978 the Fedayeen launched 2,174 operations. While an estimated 172 guerrillas were lost,[43] there was no evidence that Fedayeen attacks were more than an irritant to the regime, no suggestion that their efforts were likely to ignite the expected 'people's revolution'. Indeed the organisation's lack of success prompted a debate on strategy which produced a minority split. In 1976 this affiliated with the Tudeh, denouncing the theory of 'propaganda by the deed'.

While the Fedayeen did gain the passive support of large numbers of young people, who applauded their efforts in offering some form of opposition to the state, they had adopted a strategy which placed them wholly outside the workers' movement. Rural guerrilla warfare and 'propaganda by the deed' merely reproduced the substitutionist politics of the Tudeh tradition. The Tudeh anticipated that the 'progressive bourgeoisie' and petit bourgeoisie could play a key role in change. The new left maintained that guerrilla activists and peasants could play a similar part. Both were wrong: when the strike wave broke, with workers leading their own struggles, both were outside the movement, ill-equipped to understand events and helpless to influence them.

The Mojahedin

The guerrilla Mojahedin found itself in an almost identical position. While its approach was superficially different, it had also inherited much of the Tudeh tradition.

The organisation's origins were in the bourgeois National Front and its offshoot, the Liberation Movement. Its founders were stimulated by the failure of the Front during and after the uprising of 1963; they argued that the Front was conservative, with a leadership incapable of acting decisively, even when the regime was in crisis. They maintained that in seeking a new leadership for the opposition movement the key role should be allocated to religious leaders who had played a 'progressive' role during the 1963 events. The special character of Iranian Shiism – its 'revolutionary' dimension – should be fully recognised.

They also expressed the anti-imperialist sentiments which were being voiced by the young critics of the Tudeh who established the Fedayeen. Like them, the founders of the Mojahedin were stimulated by events in Cuba, in Algeria and in Vietnam. Such national liberation struggles were a model on which a successful struggle against the Pahlavis could be based, they argued, maintaining that objective conditions in Iran were ripe for change but that effective revolutionary leadership was absent. What was needed was a new armed leadership for the opposition movement.

Developing such a leadership became a preoccupation , with early leaders of the Mojahedin, such as Saeed Mohsen, concentrating on the establishment of a close-knit clandestine organisation capable of resisting the regime's efforts to infiltrate the opposition.

During the early years there was little theoretical development of this position. The group's members assumed that a more radical version of the National Front leadership – including guerrilla leaders and religious figures – would be capable of leading a mass movement and that change would follow. But by the late 1960s, as the influence of radical nationalism penetrated the whole opposition, the Mojahedin leadership developed an analysis of Iranian society which paralleled that of the Fedayeen.

The Mojahedin argued that Iran had come under the influence of Western imperialism, especially the US, and that as the country had been transformed from a 'bourgeois-feudal' to a 'bourgeois-*comprador*' system the main enemy was now the local agent of imperialism, the *comprador* class. The principal task of revolutionaries, they maintained, was to destabilise the regime by breaking up the police network – the Shah's main weapon in controlling the opposition movement. Armed struggle was required, combining urban and guerrilla warfare, but it was also necessary to recognise that in Iranian conditions the mass of the people could also be activated by use of what the organisation believed to be the 'revolutionary' currents within Shiism. Drawing on the tradition of theologians such as Ali Shariati, they maintained that the Prophet Muhammad had been a revolutionary and the history of the faith one of unending struggle against unjust rulers.

The Mojahedin also began military operations in 1971 and until the outbreak of the revolution in 1978 conducted hundreds of guerrilla attacks, losing large numbers of activists, though not as heavily as the Fedayeen. Like the Fedayeen, they had little impact on the regime, and, while drawing on the sympathy extended to active opposition groups, had no measurable effect on the mass of the population.

As with the Fedayeen, failure to stimulate the expected mass upsurge had an effect on the organisation, producing a fierce debate over acceptability of the Marxist method and its relationship to Islamic teachings. Formally, the Mujahedin argued that their inspiration was Islamic and that while they 'respected' Marxism they rejected the materialist method. But leading members attempted a synthesis of Islam and Marxism; in a document issued in 1975 – 'An Answer to the Regime's Latest Slanders' – they argued that:

In the whole of the Koran there is not a single Muslim who was not a revolutionary ... The regime is trying to place a wedge between Muslims and Marxists. In our view, however, there is only one major enemy – imperialism and its local collaborators ... in the present situation there is organic unity between Muslim revolutionaries and Marxist revolutionaries. In truth, why do we respect Marxism? Of course, Marxism and Islam are not identical. Nevertheless, Islam is definitely closer to Marxism than to Pahlavism. Islam and Marxism teach the same lessons, for they fight against injustice...[44]

The majority of the leadership announced that it had embraced Marxism and that henceforth the organisation should be also be viewed as 'Marxist-Leninist'. They declared that Islam was 'the ideology of the middle class', while Marxism was 'the salvation of the working class'. But those sections of the organisation with close links to the *bazaar* and to religious leaders rejected the shift and the Mojahedin split into 'Marxist' and Islamic wings.

The Mojahedin 'Marxists' and the Fedayeen now conducted unsuccessful negotiations for fusion, the Mojahedin group remaining an independent organisation which later became *Peykar* ('Combat').[45]

Trapped by tradition

When the mass movement emerged in 1978 all the opposition organisations were paralysed. The National Front and Liberation Movement expressed bourgeois interests, were hostile to independent workers' activity and incapable of influencing the strike movement. But in the case of the Tudeh and the guerrilla organisations – formally committed to revolutionary mass action – their ineffectiveness was a result of the substitutionist traditions each had inherited. Collectively, the left had abandoned the working class, substituting the 'progressive bourgeoisie', the petit bourgeoisie, the peasantry and armed resistance as agents of change. As a result, except in the rarest cases, the left was absent from the strike movement. It had no immediate audience and no influence.

This did not prevent workers initiating strike action; it did not inhibit the wide spread of the strikes nor their shift from economic to political issues – all these aspects of the movement were a function of the working class's spontaneous move into collective action. But there was no workers' organisation to call for the widening and deepening of the strike committees, their co-ordination across industry, and their generalisation as the highest level of workers' struggle. Despite the existence of a huge and eager audience seeking a way forward for the movement, there was only one voice to be heard at a national level – that of the clergy.

Socialists cannot create workers' councils – they emerge from the mass strike as an expression of collective action. But under circumstances of rising struggle, the presence of a socialist organisation committed to workers' democracy has its own impact, co-ordinating the efforts of militant workers and helping to generalise the efforts of the most advanced sections of the working class. At its highest level, this means that a revolutionary party can lead the working class in its attempt to seize power in the interests of the majority of society. In 1917 the Bolsheviks were able to argue for 'All Power to the *Soviets*.' Alas, in 1978 there was no socialist organisation within the Iranian workers' movement to call even for co-ordination of the strike committees.

The clergy profited enormously from workers' inability to develop a strategy based upon their own power. Khomeini's task became far easier: despite the fact that real power lay in the factories, his supporters could exercise growing influence from the streets. Absence of leadership within the strike movement produced a political vacuum – but this was something that could not last for long. It was soon filled by ideas alien to the interests of the working class – a call for the leadership of Khomeini and the establishment of the 'Islamic Republic'. The clergy's strategy for the revolution was successful by default.

3: After the Shah

BY JANUARY 1979 the Shah was gone and Khomeini was preparing to return to Tehran in triumph. The ayatollah was widely accepted as leader of the mass movement and was already using his position to try to control the radical elements within it. He had been happy to encourage the strikers when concerted pressure on the Shah was needed – by late January he was preparing to destroy them.

On 20 January he established the Committee for Co-ordination and Investigation of Strikes (CCIS). This was composed of bourgeois opponents of the Shah – Bazargan, Sanjabi and Moinfar – and the religious leaders Bahonar and Rafsanjani. Their task was 'to call off those strikes which jeopardise the work of the main industries involved in the production of people's urgent needs, and those threatening the country's survival.' Within ten days – three weeks before the insurrection which removed the Bakhtiar government – the CCIS had succeeded in persuading 118 striking workplaces and some public services back to work.[1]

This was a index of the increasing influence of the religious leadership, though the mullahs still did not dominate the strike movement. Despite a CCIS instruction to the railway strike committee to carry fuel 'for the consumption of the people', the strikers refused on several occasions. Customs workers declared they would release only vital goods, while the oil workers repeatedly rebuffed CCIS attempts to re-start production, one of their leaders resigning and publishing a declaration which attack-ed the 'repression' by Khomeini's representatives.[2]

But the disputes were a warning of what was to come once Khomeini and his supporters were formally in control. They showed that with the Shah gone the contradictory nature of the protest movement would rapidly be exposed, that despite the strike committees' importance they did not lead the movement, indeed that the movement was under the influence of forces alien to working class interests.

'The revolution is over'

By mid-February, the Bakhtiar government was on the brink. Despite the clergy's attempt to hold back the movement on the grounds that Khomeini had not issued instructions for armed confrontation, the insurrection in Tehran broke the back of the regime. This was soon followed by the destruction of the Pahlavi state apparatus – but while the police, the courts, *Savak* and sections of the armed forces disintegated, the fabric of Iranian capitalism was largely untouched.

The contradiction in the movement was evident. When Bakhtiar fell on 11 February, Khomeini appointed a Provisional Government. The bourgeois liberal Bazargan, a founder of the Liberation Movement, was named prime minister. His cabinet was made up of representatives of the bourgeosie and petit bourgeoisie acceptable to Khomeini. It was, wrote Shaul Bakhash,

> ...a cabinet of engineers, lawyers, educators, doctors, and former civil servants, men drawn from the professional middle class and the broad centre of Iranian politics. The majority had pursued successful careers. A number headed prosperous engineering or business firms.[3]

The new government represented that section of Iranian capital unscathed by the revolution – plus the aspirant petit bourgeoisie which hoped to gain from the upheaval. Despite six months of mass strikes and factory occupations these social layers still dominated the Iranian system. Some employers and man-agers had gone into hidding or fled the country but many remained: they had supported the opposition movement, were not compromised by direct association with the regime, or were protected by their links with the mosque or individual religious leaders. In addition, the *bazaar* was not only intact but had greatly expanded its influence. In the countryside, though some landlords had fled, many remained, leaving political relations little changed.

The new government was immediately charged with returning the country to economic normality – in effect, consolidating the control of the social layers it represented. Meanwhile, the main object of its attention – the strike committees – held control in hundreds of workplaces. But nowhere were the committees moving towards a co-ordinated attack on the structure of the capitalist system.

The protest movement had originated as a response to the crisis of the Iranian system and its forms of struggle were those dictated by the structures of capitalism – but its leadership was not anti-capitalist. The national leadership's aim had been to modify the system by removing a ruling group which had refused it a share in power – when this was accomplished its concern was to put an end to the movement from below, which threatened the gains already made.

The bourgeoisie and petit bourgeoisie had remained within the opposition movement far longer than in 1951-53, when the threat from the working class had led them to re-align with the Shah and his Western backers. Twenty-five years later, despite the advances they had made under the Pahlavis, sections of these classes had been so alienated by the Shah's policies that they believed they had more to gain from his removal. They also felt confident in a religious leadership with which they had much in common and which seemed capable of influencing the working class in a way which even the Tudeh had not been capable of doing under Mossadeq.

Under these conditions the new government prepared for an all-out offensive against the very forces that had made the revolution. With the ejection of Bakhtiar it launched a new form of class war – one directed against the mass movement. Bazargan's spokesman, Abbas Amir-Entezam, was precise about its intentions. He insisted:

Those who imagine the revolution continues are mistaken. The revolution is over. The period of reconstruction has begun.[4]

'A riot of democracy'

But millions believed that the revolution had just started. The fall of the Shah and then of Bakhtiar produced a surge of confidence and, as in the early 1950s, there was a sense of liberation which stimulated demands for further radical change. Everywhere there was a rapid extension of popular power:

> Security had collapsed. The officers and the rank and file in the army, national police and gendarmerie in major towns and centres had abandoned their barracks, police stations and posts. The citizenry was in control of barracks and police stations, palaces and ministries. In government offices, private companies, factories and universities, employees, in a riot of participatory democracy, were demanding to be consulted on policies and appointments. Army units refused to accept commanders appointed by the provisional government; newly-appointed police chiefs were arrested by citizens' committees; governors found the way to their offices barred by revolutionary youths.[5]

The weight of the religious leadership was still not enough to restrain the masses. As in so many of the great mass movements – the 1917 revolution in Russia, the Spanish revolution of 1936, the Portuguese revolution of 1974, the Polish uprising of 1980 – people who had been oppressed for generations were expressing a new sense of freedom. While the government was committed to 'consolidation', everywhere the masses were raising the level of collective action.

This took many forms. There was a flood of publishing: with *Savak* and the censors gone, newspapers, magazines, leaflets and posters appeared in huge numbers. Even the classical texts of Marxist literature were freely available for the first time in a generation. Meetings – in the streets, in schools and universities – debated politics, history, religion and culture. Hitherto largely silent sections of the population produced a stream of new ideas and organisations: most prominent were the women's organisations, with their demands for equal rights.

In the countryside peasants began seizing the land. In Gorgan and Gonbad peasant councils were formed which began to cultivate on a communal basis. Meanwhile, among the national minorities which together made up more than half the population, there were demands for autonomy. In Kurdistan, Baluchistan, Sistan, Khuzistan and Turkoman Sarai there were calls for linguistic freedom, an independent press and and the right to form independent political organisations.

Most important, the workers' movement reached new levels of activity. During the first weeks of the Provisional Government an estimated 50,000 workers were engaged in new strikes – a pattern repeated for almost six months. In the 12 months from February 1979 there were more than 350 separate industrial disputes.[6] There were demands for the payment of delayed wages and against employers' lock-outs and lay-offs, and new occupations of workplaces where owners had fled or been declared bankrupt. Here the strike committees took control.

Most of the strikes on economic issues were successful. News of progress in one factory led to new demands and strikes in others – there were waves of disputes in the main industrial areas. As a result, in 1979 as a whole the average wage rose by 53 per cent, while the minimum wage for unskilled labourers more than doubled.[7]

There were also numerous struggles for improvements in working conditions and for the establishment of welfare services. Canteens, sports facilities, clinics, insurance schemes and even provisions for workplace education were extracted from employers – something formerly unthinkable. In those workplaces where management had fled, workers took control of the production process – they not only regulated the pace of work but began to organise the buying of raw materials and the sale of products. There was a genuine measure of 'workers' control' over production and administration.[8]

Throughout the country the organ of control was the council or *shora*. Peasants established *shoras* to organise collective work on the land, while there were attempts at 'neighbourhood *shoras*' in some areas.[9] In schools, universities and even in the armed forces, *shoras* mushroomed. But the real home of the *shora* was in industry, where the councils gave a new dimension to the workers' movement. This new-found strength was a direct challenge to the forces of reaction grouped in the Provisional Government.

A process of permanent revolution was again unfolding. The bourgeoisie and petit bourgeoisie had discovered the point at which their own interests were under threat. Incapable of advancing the process of change, whether in the cities, on the land, or among the national minorities, they were now committed to 'reconstruction', an attempt to stabilise their own rule. The pattern of the Mossadeq years was at last being repeated: while the bourgeoisie discovered the limits of its ambition, the most advanced sections of society demanded further change. The next, most crucial phase of the revolution centred on the Provisional Government's efforts to smash the most powerful elements within the mass movement – the workers' *shoras*.

Workers' control and the power of the *shoras*

The *shoras* expressed a new level of working-class activity and consciousness. They were based upon the strike committees of the earlier period of the revolution, but were more formal bodies. In general, they operated as committees directly elected by the workforce, though the precise structure varied according to the size of the workplace and the type of industry, the nature of the production process, the form of ownership, the record of militancy, especially in the early months of the revolution, and the political orientation of leading activists.

According to Bayat:

> ...successful *shoras* were those which exerted full control over and ran the workplace without any effective control on the part of the officially-appointed managers. Their politics and activities were independent of the state and the official managers and were based upon the interests of the rank and file workers.[10]

When *shoras* operated in this way they controlled not only finance, administration and management but took over the 'security' functions formerly carried out by *Savak* and the army. At the Fanoos factory, an example of the most advanced organisation, these rights were enshrined in the *shora*'s constitution, giving the council authority to organise groups of workers to deal with 'counter-revolutionary sabotage', military training and 'the purge of corrupt, anti-popular and idle elements, in any position'. When managers or workers were indicted by the committee, they came before a full mass meeting which voted on their fate.[11]

It was when the *shoras* operated in this fashion that they were most likely to raise general political issues and to co-ordinate activity. In those areas with the most activist and democratic *shoras*, links across workplaces were established. The Union of Workers' *Shoras* of Gilan and the Union of Workers' *Shoras* of Western Tehran provided a basic level of co-ordination between separate workplace councils. There was a national-link-up of railway workers, while in the oilfields the *shoras* met to discuss issues such as the level of production and even the pricing of crude oil for export.

Meanwhile, the office of the Shah's *Savak*-controlled unions in Tehran was occupied by unemployed workers and renamed *Khaneh Kargar* – Workers' House. Here, workers' councils and committees could hold meetings and co-ordinate activity.

Such co-ordination reached its highest level with the establishment of the Founding Council of the All-Iran Workers' Union. This body showed that the *shoras* were stimulating generalisation above the level of the workplace and the industrial group and were doing so at a national level. On 1 March 1979 it issued a declaration which asserted:

> We the workers of Iran, through our strikes, sit-ins and demonstrations overthrew the Shah's regime and during these months of strike we tolerated unemployment, poverty and even hunger. Many of us were killed in the struggle. We did all this in order to create an Iran free of class repression, free of exploitation. We made the revolution in order to end unemployment and homelessless, to replace the *Savak*-oriented syndicates with independent workers' *shoras* – *shoras* formed by the workers of each factory for their own economic and political needs.[12]

Its 24-point programme included demands for a 40-hour week, longer holidays, sick pay, tax-free bonuses, and free canteens and health services at work. It also called for government recognition of the *shoras*, the freedom to demonstrate and the right to strike, and the expulsion of all foreign experts and capitalists and the appropriation of their capital in the interest of the workers.

This national body – and the regional co-ordinating councils – were the most advanced bodies proooduced by the revolution. In the most militant areas – Gilan, Tehran and the Khuzistan oilfield – they were proto-*soviets*, organisations which expressed the interests of the most advanced groups of workers, with an understanding of the need to carry the movement beyond the individual workplace. But still they did not generalise the interests of the class as a whole and like the strike committees of earlier months they did not develop into fully-fledged organs of workers' power.

The battle for the *shoras*

In response to the growing militancy of the working class and the spread of the *shoras*, the Provisional Government adopted a two-pronged strategy: whille it attempted to salvage industry, commerce and finance, it spared no effort in its attempt to destroy the workers' movement.

In a move designed to plug the gaps left by fleeing employers and managers, and those businessmen who had been declared bankrupt, the new regime nationalised 483 production units as well as banks and insurance companies. This was not an attempt to bring industry under state control for ideological reasons but to strengthen the badly-weakened structure of Iranian capitalism, which, the government understood, needed swift attention. New managers were appointed to run the plants and offices.[13]

Meanwhile a direct assault on the *shora* movement was under way. Three days after the insurrection, Khomeini instructed all strikers to return to work. A month later, when it had become clear that new strikes were spreading and *shoras* were being established everywhere, the government issued a new statement. This declared:

> Any disobedience from, and sabotage of the implementation of the plans of the Provisional Government will be regarded as opposition against the genuine Islamic Revolution. The provocateurs and agents will be introduced to people as counter-revolutionary elements, so that the nation will decide about them, as they did about

the counter-revolutionary regime of the Shah.[14]

But still the *shoras* could not be halted. According to one survey of industry, while the number of workplaces making new demands for improved pay and conditions remained steady throughout the spring, political demands of the most advanced workers became more insistent.[15] *Shoras* showed no sign of complying with the government, which now stepped up the pace of its offensive.

In May it introduced the Law of Special Force to prevent *shoras* intervening 'in the affairs of the managements and of the appointments' of government-nominated managers.[16] In June, the new constitution also attempted to restrict the activity of the *shoras*. According to Articles 104 and 105, they were to be composed of 'representatives of workers, peasants, other employeees, and the managers, in the productive, industrial and agricultural units.' In addition, 'decisions taken by the *shoras* must not be against Islamic principles and the country's laws.'[17]

Even these measures did not diminish enthusiasm for the councils. In June and July the pace of struggle accelerated until more industrial units were raising demands than in February, when the mass movement had been renewed after the fall of the Bakhtiar government. But suddenly, in mid-summer, a retreat began. The number of factories raising new demands fell sharply – according to Bayat from 67 to a mere 14. By August the total had dropped to just five. The regime had reversed the tide and in many workplaces, *shoras* were forced on to the defensive. The six months after the insurrection had been the crucial period; from mid-summer the government seized the initiative and Khomeini – as determined to destroy the movement as he had been to remove the Shah – never let go.

A number of objective factors aided the government's offensive on the councils. One was the collapse of some areas of industry. Even before the protest movement broke in 1978, the Shah's policy had produced dislocation in some key areas, with bankruptcies and closures. When mass political strikes began in October 1978 businessmen who feared the movement had sold off or broken up their holdings; others had distributed their raw materials or finished products among *bazaaris;* records had been removed and destroyed.

In addition, the events of 1978 had interrupted the flow of raw materials and machinery into the country, with serious results for an economy in which much industrial production depended upon imports. Thus in 1977-78 raw materials and semi-finished goods worth $5.6 billion were imported. By 1978-79 the figure had fallen to $3.9 billion and by 1979-80, to $3.8 billion. Imports of equipment for industry fell by two-thirds over two years: imports of capital goods for industry were worth $2.5 billion in 1977-78 but only $1 billion by 1979-80.[18]

By the spring of 1979 these pressures were taking their toll on the working class. Production in most industrial plants fell steeply and despite the strength of the strike committees and later the *shoras*, unemployment rocketed. Demonstrations of unemployed workers took place in several cities and in Tehran the ministries of labour and justice and the former *Savak* offices (now *Khaneh Kargar*) were occupied by protestors demanding work.

Despite the unity of employed and unemployed workers – evident in a huge 1 May demonstration in Tehran – the rising level of unemployment had its impact on workplace organisation.

But in the battle for control of the workplaces, it was the character of the *shora* movement and especially the nature of its political leadership that was decisive. When Khomeini's Provisional Government began its assault on the working class it was assisted by the fact that the *shora* movement was far from homogeneous. The most advanced *shoras* were democratic bodies, drawing their authority from mass meetings, subject to recall and open to radical and socialist ideas – by this stage some sections of the left had recognised the importance of the *shoras* and were attempting, with mixed results, to influence them.

But other *shoras* were run on a far less open basis. Where managers remained, these *shoras* co-operated with them or with government appointees sent in under the nationalisation measures. And in that minority of *shoras* in which leading activists were enthusiastic supporters of the mullahs, there was liaison between the council and government to the extent that the *shora* worked to dismiss secular managers and install so-called *maktabi* loyalist managements, which backed the regime. The government could thus attack the *shora* movement from within.

But pro-regime *shoras* were in a tiny minority and the Provisional Government needed other allies inside the workplaces. It found these among the technicians, production managers and supervisors. This layer was an important part of the new petit bourgeoisie which had emerged over the preceding 20 years and was essentially conservative. As in many semi-industrial countries it was relatively well-educated, highly paid and had little in common with the shopfloor workers. Before the revolution it had operated as an agency of bourgeois and state interests in industry. Many of its members now opposed the Shah but saw the purpose of the opposition movement as modifying the system to better express their own interests. The Provisional Government reflected just these petit bourgeois aspirations.

With rare exceptions the technicians obstructed the *shoras*. They refused to use their specialist skills to continue or restart production, supported pro-regime, *maktabi* managements or government representatives, and backed the activities of the most reactionary *shoras* – those seeing themselves as an expression of the government's will. As the regime brought greater pressure on the *shora* movement and it became clear that the workers had no overall strategy of their own, the technicians became more confident and were able to erode the position of some worker militants.

Most *shoras* represented the whole workforce – manual workers, administrative staff and the technical grades. This meant that in some workplaces the technicians could be a bridge between the workforce and management. Where the shopfloor was relatively weak, or the *shora* acted as mainly as a 'consultative' body, the technicians and supervisors could be decisive. In these workplaces, management saw the *shora* as a method of incorporating activists – and the technicians made the process of bureaucratisation of some militants much easier.

But there was another dimension to the struggle taking place inside the *shoras*. Unlike the strike committees, which had been produced by the mass action of the 1978 movement, the *shoras* developed under conditions in which the workers' movement was under attack from the leadership of the revolution. Once confident that he could oust the Shah, Khomeini had set out to destroy the workers' movement. His supporters in the *shoras* were at first marginal but as time passed they became more influential – their impact in each workplace being a function of the degree of political development of the workers' movement nationally and of the leading local activists.

The experience of the strike movement was now repeated, for Khomeini's influence in the workplaces increased largely because of the absence of a coherent political alternative, and, where secular organisations did offer new strategies, as a result of their inadequacy.

The left commits suicide

All the organisations of the Iranian left developed in a tradition which had revised Marxism, seeing forces other than the working class as the agents of revolutionary change. This substitutionism meant that during the mass strikes of 1978 all these organisations were marginal. But during the insurrection of February the guerrilla organisations had their moment – the Fedayeen and Mojahedin playing the leading role in assaulting loyalist strongholds in Tehran and breaking the back of the Shah's state. Conditions then moved sharply in favour of the left. The 'riot of democracy' was in full swing, with the workers', women's, peasants' and national minority movements setting the pace. Fevered debates were taking place in every area of Iranian society and potentially the left had a huge audience.

For the first time since the early 1950s the left could organise openly. Conditions were particularly favourable during the first four months after the insurrection, when the workers' movement was on the offensive. The level of workers' self-confidence is demonstrated by the hundreds of workplaces raising new demands and the repeated demonstrations and rallies which took up workers' issues.[19] These reached a climax on May Day when a huge parade filled Tehran – among an estimated one and half million people were many factory delegations and large groups of unemployed workers carrying banners inscribed with slogans which reflected the demands of the most advanced workers: 'Nationalisation of all industries', 'There is no kind capitalist in the world', 'Long live real unions and real *shoras*', 'Equal wages for women and men', 'Work for the unemployed'.[20]

But in practice the audience of the left was less among workers than among university and school students and professionals. Here the Fedayeen and Mojahedin had their roots and could attract large numbers – indeed they became the main pole of attraction among the secular organisations; the pulling power of the Fedayeen being illustrated by their ability to attract 150,000 to a rally called at Tehran University in late February. The Tudeh, too, won fresh interest on the basis that it was the traditional opposition to the Shah, though as we shall see, it did not attract those who looked for an alternative to the new regime.

Belatedly recognising the significance of the workers' movement, some guerrilla activists attempted to influence the *shoras*. There were isolated successes: at the important Chit-e Jahan factory at Karaj, for example, which had a long history of political activism, there was strong Mojahedin influence on the workers' council.[21] Elsewhere individual workers were attracted by the guerrillas and helped to give them small audiences among militants. But these were exceptions which proved the rule: nowhere did the guerrillas have a firm base in industry and nowhere did they have an opportunity to influence the direction of the *shora* movement. But this was only half the problem – the real difficulty was that the left did not understand the significance of the *shoras*. As Bayat comments:

> Almost all of the left was surprised by the sudden emergence of the *shoras*. Almost all the left-wing organisations, as well as the *shoras* themselves, were confused about what to do and about what kind of possible role the *shoras* could play politically.[22]

Thus even where the left had contact with worker militants it had little to say about the direction of the *shora* movement. On the most important development of the revolutionary experience the left was silent – or worse, offered negative advice. For the left did have ideas about the way forward for the mass movement as a whole – ideas which soon proved suicidal.

For the Tudeh, the Provisional Government merited uncritical support and the party liquidated its members into the movement around Khomeini. For the guerrilla organisations of the 'new left' the situation was more complicated; they were not only disoriented by the character of the mass movement but adopted equivocal attitudes towards the Provisional Government. Thus even where the guerrillas were able to influence individuals in the workers' movement they could not offer a perspective which expressed working-class interests.

The disorientation shown by all the organisations was a result of the tradition in which each was rooted. Each had pursued strategies directed away from the working class. When the Shah fell, these propelled them towards the workers' most determined enemies – the bourgeoisie and petit bourgeosie.

Why, at the most important moment in modern Iranian history, did the left insist on maintaining such an approach?

The tragedy of Stalinism

The Tudeh, and later the guerrillas, had developed in a tradition which led them to abandon the working class as the agency of revolutionary change. The result was that at the highest point of the revolutionary movement they were unable to distinguish their class enemies. This was a problem which had dogged the left since the degeneration of the communist movement in the 1920s.

After the isolation of the Russian revolution in the early 1920s and the emergence of a new ruling bureaucracy in Russia, the Communist International (Comintern) entered a period during which it became no more than an arm of Moscow's foreign policy. By the late 1920s it was imposing a set of strategic principles on the international communist movement which reflected the priorities of Russian state capitalism but had little to do with the needs of the world working class. It insisted that in a relatively backward country such as Iran any idea of independent working class action was a nonsense: that the principle guiding the activity of communists must be the need to form a 'class bloc' which could assist the 'democratic forces' present in such countries.

The idea of the class bloc was imposed on communist parties in the backward regions of the world as part of a package of ideas which included a number of already bankrupt theories. Among these was the notion that in countries less developed than the industrialised states of Europe and North America, socialist revolution was impossible. Rather, it was argued, social change would proceed through 'stages', the first of which, in countries dominated by the imperial powers, would be a 'democratic' stage. During this phase, the bourgeoisie would lead a struggle to free the nation from the imperialist yoke and establish democratic rights – such as universal suffrage, a parliament, freedom of association and a free press – similar to those enjoyed in the advanced capitalist states. Only when this stage had been attained, it was argued, would it be possible for the working class to advance towards the prospect of a revolutionary change from capitalism to socialism.

Such an approach had been understandable in the years before the Russian revolution. Then, the majority of revolutionaries, including the Bolsheviks themselves under Lenin's leadership, had accepted variants of the stages theory, despite Trotsky's insistence that the experiencee of the Russian revolution of 1905 proved that only the proletariat – the industrial working class – could make a revolution in the backward countries. In 1917 Trotsky's approach, which he termed 'permanent revolution', was vindicated as the bourgeoisie vacillated and collapsed, the working class showing itself to be the only force capable of bringing change. At this point Lenin was won to Trotsky's analysis of the permanent revolution. He then convinced the Bolsheviks of the necessity for a working class struggle for power. Lenin and Trotsky led the party in its effort to convince workers that their *soviets* were the basis for an assault on the state and the establishment of a new order.

After the October Revolution, in which the workers of Russia destroyed the remnants of the Tsarist state, the idea of permanent revolution in the backward countries became a Bolshevik principle and a tenet of the Communist International. Only when the Comintern started to degenerate under the influence of Stalin and Russia's new state-capitalist ruling group was this principle abandoned. By the late 1920s the Russian bureaucracy had achieved power in the face of a scattered, weakened and demoralised working class among which *soviet* democracy had become a fiction, and it now developed a new set of principles for the international communist movement. Resolved to pursue the counter-revolutionary project of 'socialism in one country', Stalin's party sought bourgeois allies abroad and a theoretical structure which would legitimise its policy.[23]

This new policy discovered 'progressive' elements of the bourgeoisie under circumstances which the theory of permanent revolution and the experience of the October revolution had long since ruled out. It reasserted theories in which forces other than the working class could play a 'revolutionary' role, directing communists to participate alongside them. In short, the Stalinist conception of change removed the working class from the centre of the political stage, placing other classes and blocs of classes in its place.

The results of the policy were catastrophic. In 1925, it was 'rehearsed' in China. Moscow instructed the Chinese Communist Party to participate in a front with the bourgeois nationalist Kuomintang, despite the activity of a mass workers' movement, in order to support a nationalist leadership which Stalin hoped to make into a reliable ally. The policy was justified on the basis that China was about to pass through the 'democratic' phase of change and that the bourgeoisie should be supported by the workers' and peasants' movements – which themselves should raise only limited demands. The theses of permanent revolution were ignored. Predictably, within months the Kuomintang had destroyed much of the workers' movement and murdered thousands of Chinese communists.[24]

Despite this disaster and subsequent changes of line in Comintern policy, the idea of a 'bloc' of progressive classes and the notion that any social revolution needed to pass through the 'democratic' stage were elevated to strategic principles, together with the related idea of the 'Popular Front', which when implemented in Europe caused further disasters, notably in Germany and Spain.[25]

The Communist Party of Iran (CPI), which looked to the Comintern for its strategic principles, was much affected by these policies. During the late 1920s, Moscow's desire to come to an accomodation with Reza Shah had been a serious blow to CPI members and the party effectively collapsed. Subsequently, Iranians who looked to Moscow for guidance were enjoined to seek out sections of those 'progressive' classes with whom they could form an appropriate bloc against the regime and its Western backers. While there was a break between the disintegration of the CPI and the formation of the Tudeh in 1941, leftists who remained active during the 1930s, such as the famous 'Fifty-three' arrested in 1937, who later formed the nucleus of the Tudeh, all developed their political ideas in the Stalinist context.[26]

The Tudeh declined to declare itself a Marxist organisation but bore all the hallmarks of a party operating within the framework laid down by Moscow. It argued that the left must guard against the danger of 'premature' revolution, as shown by the experience in Spain, and that Iran was not ready for such radical change.[27] The main task, the party argued, was that of weakening the ruling class by 'uniting all progressive forces'. It announced a reformist programme directed towards 'the masses', among which it included intellectuals, small landowners, crafts-men-traders and government employees.

This was the policy which, despite the favourable conditions of the 1940s and early 1950s, led the Tudeh to disaster in 1953. Then, arguing for the need to form a 'progressive bloc' with liberal capitalists and to carry through the 'democratic stage' of the revolution, the Tudeh had abandoned the workers' movement and watched while the Shah's imperialist allies rescued a relieved bourgeoisie.

The defeat of 1953 led young critics of the Tudeh to develop the current which, almost 20 years later, produced the Fedayeen. For these activists the rejection of the party's passivity and the launching of an armed struggle marked a sharp break with the old tradition. But the founders of the Fedayeen had not broken with the Tudeh's Stalinist heritage, they had merely modified it. Most important, they had absorbed the fundamental flaw in the Stalinist method – the substitution of other forces for the working class.

Fedayeen founders such as Pouyan argued that in the absence of workers' struggle the task of socialists was to begin an armed struggle. This would break the deadlock on the left, allowing the re-groupment of 'revolutionary elements' and would shock the masses into activity, precipitating an upsurge which would threaten the regime. The principal role in stimulating revolutionary change thus lay with the guerrilla.

This was the crudest form of the substitutionism which was at the centre of the Fedayeen strategy, replacing the activity of the workers' movement with that of the fighter. But the politics of the Fedayeen incorporated another and more complex idea which also drew on the traditions of the Tudeh and reinforced the substitutionist core of their strategy. This was the notion of the system of 'dependent capitalism'.

This theory had become well established by the 1960s as the ideas of the 'Latin-American' school became popular on the left in both the advanced capitalist countries and the 'Third World'. It emphasised the dependent status of countries outside the capitalist heartlands of Western Europe and North America and the imperialist strategy of developing a *comprador* class within those states they had subordinated. Such a class, usually built around the local representatives of Western multinationals, it was argued, became an agent of imperial capital. It was profoundly reactionary, unlike the 'national bourgeoisie', a class seen as having roots in the indigenous economy and which was hostile to the rule of foreign capital.

The task of revolutionaries in Third World countries, argued the 'dependency' theorists, was to secure a 'people's alliance' between the workers, the peasants, the national bourgeoisie and other progressive elements – one aimed at challenging the power of the *comprador* class and hence imperial hegemony.

One of the Fedayeen's most influential documents, written by its leading theorist, Bizan Jazani, explained how the theory should be applied under Iranian conditions. **The Socio-Economic Analysis of a Dependent Capitalist State** was published in 1973. This maintained that during the decade of the 1960s the *comprador* bourgeoisie had come to dominate Iran, a result of 'the channelling of the bourgeoisie towards *comprador* capitalism, the dissolution of feudalism, the fragmentation of the small bourgeoisie and the polarisation of the petit bourgeoisie'.[28] Iranian revolutionaries were thus faced with the task of uniting all 'progressive' classes – the workers, peasants, intelligentsia, progressive petit bourgeoisie and national capitalists – against the *comprador* class.

Jazani was quite explicit about the consequences of his analysis. He argued:

Since the relations of production in this system are based on capitalism, there seems to be a tendency among some Marxist elements to believe that the principal contradiction in Iran today is that between capital and labour. If this is the case then our country is on the verge of a socialist revolution and the working class together with its allies forms the basis of the revolution. But this is an erroneous belief ... the contradiction between labour and capital, with its social manifestation of a confrontation between the proletarian and the bourgeoisie, cannot be the principal contradiction of the system prevailing in Iran. For this reason our society is not at the stage of a socialist revolution, ie it is not a revolution where the slogan would be the abolition of private ownership of the means of production and the expropriation of all private capital. Moreover, the need for the reconstruction of the national economy, and the need to uproot dependent industries and to end the economic domination of imperialism immediately after the people's triumph make it imperative that our society should go through a necessary period of transition before the establishment of socialism.[29]

Jazani recognised that there was a 'contradiction' in the people's movement against the *comprador* class, that the working class did not share fundamental interests with the 'national' bourgeoisie. However, he argued, it had more in common with the latter than with the *comprador* class and its imperialist backers. As a result the workers should participate in the overall national struggle but should also sustain 'positive and active rivalry' within the liberation movement.

The dependency theory was a modified form of the theory of stages and of the need for the class bloc. It also relegated the working class to a secondary role, as a mere element in a people's liberation front. Riddled with contradictions at every level it was particularly inappropriate under Iranian conditions. The Fedayeen argued that Iran had been transformed, during the boom of the 1960s, by the massive influx of foreign capital. At this level, too, they were wrong. By the late 1960s just 90 foreign companies had invested in Iran, and while giants like Mercedes-Benz had made major investments, many were small. Even at the height of the oil boom, when foreign capital was most attracted by the growing Iranian market, its involvement was modest. By the early 1970s the government anticipated that of $72 billion to be invested in its ambitious 1973-78 development plan, just $2.8 billion, or 4 per cent, would be foreign capital. Iran had not been transformed by foreign capital but by the rapid expansion of state investment and the emergence of a far stronger and better-integrated indigenous bourgeoisie.

The Fedayeen analysis, like all such neo-Stalinist approaches, was based on premises which distorted the real economic and social problems. The process of uneven development that had been at work since the early years of the century had produced a system in which fundamental change could only be brought about by concerted working class activity, for whatever the differences between sections of the bourgeoisie, it was united in its opposition to movements from below which might threaten its own interests.

The upsurge of workers' activity after the First World War had indicated the direction from which a challenge to the system would come – the events of the 1940s and early 1950s had confirmed it. But the Tudeh then produced the disaster of 1953 – and in the absence of a revolutionary socialist alternative its perspective was given new form in the 1960s. While the notion of 'dependency' gave new clothing to the popular front and the idea of stages, it reproduced the Stalinist analysis which had already proved such a costly failure.

By the 1960s the bourgeoisie had even more to lose from an insurgent mass movement than under Mossadeq. The 'class bloc' advocated by the dependency theorists was even less appropriate and enthusiasts such as the Fedayeen were heading for another disaster. The same was true of the Mojahedin: their Islamic orientation being combined with the very same substitutionist assumptions. And the Mojahedin were to suffer the same bloody fate.

It is not true, as Moghadam[30] has claimed, that during the 1960s and 1970s the Iranian left displayed 'a distaste for theorising'. Its problem was not contempt for ideas – rather, it was the absorption of ideas that had been tried and tested in Iran and abroad, and had failed.

4: Beginning of the end

THE STRATEGIES of the left, dictated by the Stalinist tradition, made Khomeini's task of destroying the workers' movement far easier.

The Tudeh Party openly and aggressively supported the Provisional Government on the basis that it was 'anti-imperialist'. This reflected the Stalinist obsession with the search for 'progressive' sections of the bourgeoisie and petit bourgeoisie, which the Tudeh declared could now be discerned in the ruling group around Khomeini. But it was also a result of Moscow's hope that the revolution would at last allow it to gain a strong foothold in Iran. The Tudeh acted – as it had done for decades – as an arm of Russian foreign policy. Its members thus ostentatiously backed the Bazargan government and sought leading positions in the pro-Khomeini movement. When, in late March, the Government called a referendum to confirm support for its new 'Islamic Republic', the Tudeh declared itself in favour, fully placing itself in the camp of reaction.

The 'radicals' of the Mojahedin vacillated but finally adopted essentially the same approach. In January they had issued a 'Minimum Expectation Programme' which set out their hopes for the revolution. This revealed their attachment to the theory of 'dependent capitalism' and their illusion that a deal could be struck with 'progressive' elements in the bourgeoisie. It called, for example, for the appropriation of all *comprador* investments, criticised 'irresponsible' capitalism, and argued for 'the national, anti-imperialist struggle of the country as a whole'. At a time when the strike movement was at its height, it called for the administration of factories to be carried out by a council composed of 'representatives of the councils of the workers and of the clerical personnel and representatives of the employers'.[1]

Not surprisingly, the Mojahedin failed to recognise the Provisional Government's hostility to the mass movement and the working class in particular. They thus took up a position of critical support for the new regime, expressed in the conviction that opposition to 'the line of the revolution under the leadership of Khomeini' would benefit imperialism, and offered 'conditional' support in the referendum. By so doing it announced its final abandonment of the workers' movement. Whatever influence was retained in the workplaces served only to disorient militants and blunt the effectiveness of the *shoras*.

The Fedayeen were at a loss to understand the progress of events. Many of their best activists instinctively mistrusted the religious leadership but were still oriented on the Provisional Government: a function of their obsession with theories of 'stages' and the search for 'progessive' sections of the bourgeoisie.

There were intense arguments within the organisation over the precise stage reached by the revolution and the class character of the regime. These soon came to a head over the stand to be taken in backing regional and peasants' movements against the Provisional Government. There were a number of formulations of the character of the period and the tasks ahead: these included the assertion that the movement had reached the stage of 'popular democratic revolution' and that 'the proletarian class must try to cultivate the support of the peasants and urban petit bourgeoisie' in order to destroy 'the dependent bourgeois class'. This, it was argued, would allow 'the democratic revolutionary dictatorship of workers and toilers of towns and countryside' to be established. Others maintained that now the revolution had reached the 'democratic' stage a 'class dictatorship' might be established.

None spelt out that no 'democratic' stage of the revolution could be sustained by classes alien to the mass movement; that the bourgeoisie and petit bourgeoisie were classes without 'progressive' potential; that only the working class had the capacity to carry the revolution forward. These ideas, which had been the principles of revolutionary Marxism in the years after the Russian revolution, had been lost years earlier when the Iranian left had been submerged by Stalinism. Thus the Fedayeen too sought 'progressive' elements in the bourgeoisie, though with less enthusiasm than the Tudeh or the Mojahedin. They boycotted the March referendum, in which Khomeini called for support for the Islamic Republic, but were effectively paralysed by indecision and internal dissent.[2]

The conduct of the left allowed the Government to pursue its offensive against the *shoras* without serious opposition. The Tudeh and Mojahedin supported the referendum and, by implication, the attack on the *shoras*. The Fedayeen hesitated – but hesitation at such a point was as good as abstentionism. At the moment when the workers' movement was reaching its highest level – with *shoras* spreading nationally and reaching the 'pre-*soviet*' level – the left was incapable of recognising the regime's real class character. The odds were already stacked against the working class – now the left lengthened them.

The disarray of the left strengthened the hand of pro-Khomeini elements in the workplaces. The small minority of militants who had enthusiastically supported the Provisional Government from the start grew in confidence, backed by the technicians and professionals found in many plants and offices. They led attacks on secular militants and were especially hostile towards those workers linked to the left. At the Amazon factory in Tehran, for example, one of the minority of workplaces where there was a *shora* dominated by government supporters, the council's regulations stipulated that:

> ...should the aim and intention of a *shora* member be contrary to the interests of the Islamic Republic or violate laws, and disrupt the order of the company, it will be the Islamic and canonical duty of the other members to report him to the employees through the mass meetings.[3]

With the left unable to mount coherent opposition to the government, Khomeini's supporters in such workplaces made steady progress. When the Law of Special Force was introduced in May 1979 to prevent *shora* 'interference' in management and monitor the activity of militants, the government had a growing network of workers, albeit still small, willing to destroy the councils from within. All through the spring and summer the government maintained its offensive and, as the *shora* movement began to weaken, made its decisive move into the workplaces.

Following the sharp fall in strikes in mid-summer, in September 1979 the government introduced legislation for the establishment of Islamic Associations to replace the *shoras* in each workplace. The basis for the associations was the network of Khomeini supporters whose confidence had been growing as their secular opponents gradually lost their way. This move was decisive: in the political vacuum which resulted from the absence of a class-conscious leadership in the workplaces, the regime was able to take a decisive initiative against the militants. The *shoras* never recovered. It was the end of the revolution.

The *Komitehs*

Weakening the workers' movement was a preoccupation for the government during the nine months after the insurrection. The most politically-conscious figures in the Provisional Government – notably capitalists such as Bazargan and Sanjabi – understood that a confident mass movement in industry was the biggest threat to the new regime. This did not mean that their offensive on other sections of the mass movement was any less intense: throughout the spring the movements of women, peasants and national minorities were all under attack. But the fate of the wider movement was inextricably linked to that of the working class: when the *shoras* went under, the most advanced section of the working class was defeated and the mass movement was at the mercy of the regime.

This process is seen most clearly in the government's efforts to assert control over the *komitehs*. These were extensions of the neighbourhood committees that had sprung up during the mass strikes of 1978, and in which the religious network had had strong influence. After the insurrection the *komitehs* mushroomed – an expression of the sense of liberation which had seized the masses. The numbers involved in the *komitehs* were huge and the organisations themselves were disciplined, powerful and armed. They policed neighbourhoods, arrested collaborators, ran courts and prisons, organised demonstrations, and intervened in industrial disputes.

While the mullahs were prominent in these bodies from the beginning, the *komitehs* were by no means homogeneously pro-government. In May, Bazargan criticised them for unauthorised arrests, confiscations of property, unauthorised dismissal and appointment of officials, and interference in the government's work. The *komitehs*, he said, 'turn our day into night. They upset the applecart'.[4]

It was not only the Bazargan wing of the regime – later expelled by Khomeini as the clergy took full control – which was hostile to the conduct of the *komitehs*. Revolutionary Prosecutor-General Hadavi issued a series of decrees attempting to control their activity. In April he cancelled all warrants for arrests and property confiscations issued by the *komitehs*; in May he prohibited the arrest of military personnel. Rafsanjani, close to Khomeini, declared in early summer: 'The *komitehs* will not remain for ever and must soon be dissolved'.[5]

But not for the first time Khomeini had the clearest strategy. Quickly grasping the importance of the *komitehs* and the danger of secular influence within them, he set out to tame them. In April he announced that 'the *komitehs* need purging, not dissolution'.[6] One of his most trusted supporters, Mohammed-Reza Mahdavi-Kani, head of the Tehran central *komiteh*, was put in charge. He was instructed to work towards 'the transfer of duties to the responsible government authorities, the full establishment of the authority of the Provisional Government of the Islamic Republic over affairs and the eventual dissolution of the *komitehs*'.[7]

This coincided with the move by 'radical' clerics – supporters of Khomeini's brand of Islamic autocracy – to assert themselves within the Provisional Government. Establishing the Islamic Republican Party (IRP), they attempted to diminish the influence of secular elements in the government – but more important, to marginalise the left in the *komitehs*, now their most valuable constituency. Observing the pull of secular ideas among young people who had flooded into the *komitehs*, they were anxious to develop a national organisation which would express Khomeini's ideas.

These two initiatives were vital for the new regime. The

komitehs contained all the conflicting currents present in the national arena – except that of the organised working class. Most were dominated by mullahs and bazaaris but others were influenced by the left; almost all had strong support from the masses, especially the urban poor. They were therefore a battleground on which the wider class conflicts were played out, though here, as during the mass strikes, the mullahs and their allies had an enormous advantage – they were not directly confronted with the power of organised labour. The workers and the *shoras* were confined to the workplaces. In the absence of *soviets*, the *komitehs* were exposed to the influence of workplace organisation but never dominated by it.

But success for the regime came only when the workers' movement went into retreat. As the only alternative to the central government's new class rule weakened, the left in the *komitehs* was marginalised. The process which had taken place during the mass strikes of 1978 was again evident: then, the geographically-based organisation of the neigbourhood committee had limited the influence of the workplace strike committee. Now, despite the existence of much stronger workplace organisation, the geographically-based *komiteh* was again dominant.

During each phase of the revolution one factor was of critical importance: while the religious establishment proved capable of directing sections of the movement, the secular organisations failed. Thus in the period after the fall of the Shah, the left's disorientation fed the regime's confidence. Its inability to offer a strategy for the *shoras* deepened the crisis it faced in the *komitehs*. As the workers' movement went into retreat, the regime was able to marginalise the left and the liberals in the *komitehs*. Unable to organise where the mass movement had real power, the left was doomed to fail elsewhere. Its obliteration in the countryside and later in the mountains, among the national minority movements, was inevitable.

The new state and the IRP

Once the Khomeini group went on to the offensive it moved with speed to impose control on the movement. This was achieved by the establishment of a series of new institutions, presented as extensions of the movement but directed against its radical elements.

In March the regime established the *Pasdaran* – the Revolutionary Guards. The aim was twofold – to impose discipline on the *komitehs*, bringing them into a nationally-controlled structure, and to marginalise the *komitehs'* leftist and liberal activists. Recruits for the new organisation were drawn from the regime's most loyal supporters – the *lumpen* layers who had existed on the fringes of the urban economy and the petit bourgeois elements closest to the mosque who had been the most enthusiastic pro-Khomeini activists in the *komitehs*.

At first the *Pasdaran* was a motley force; not until sent into action against Kurdish separatists in the summer did it begin to act as a more disciplined instrument of the regime. It then became Khomeini's most important agent of repression and was used to intervene directly in civilian affairs, especially in industry. Eventually the Guards were used systematically to terrorise *shora* members and to liquidate the workers' committees.

In August Khomeini created the *Jahad-e Sazandegi*, the Reconstruction Crusade. Its aim was to 'rebuild' the Iranian economy; activities included the repair of roads, maintenance of government buildings and work in the countryside. Workers were directed away from the factories to take part in these schemes – a method of breaking up the workforce, particularly in militant workplaces, and bringing activists directly under the regime's discipline. Strikes were declared illegal.

By the late summer the government was also energetically engaged in establishing Islamic *shoras* and the *Anjoman-e Islami* – the Islamic Societies designed to carry the regime's policy into the workplaces. These included members of management and of the workforce and government representatives. Acting together with Islamic *shoras*, or with the regime's supporters in more militant factories, the *Anjoman-e Islami* set out to replace *shoras* altogether.

These bodies were not expressions of the mass movement, like the *shoras*, or in a different sense, the *komitehs*. They were set up by the new regime to police the movement, to control the energies of the masses. They were the first organisational expressions of the regime's need to impose a new form of class rule.

These were the elements of a new state – or rather the bodies the new regime needed to graft on to remnants of the old state in order to consolidate its rule. While the Shah's police, courts, and prisons had been broken by the insurrection, much of the civil administration remained intact, as did large parts of the armed forces, particularly the officer corps.

The new bodies were constructed piecemeal, in response to a series of pressures – but they were not established arbitrarily. Their emergence reflected the increasing coherence of the most determined faction within the regime – that of Khomeini and his supporters. This was also expressed in the increasing prominence of the faction's own party organisation – the IRP.

The development of the IRP was vital for the Khomeini group. It enabled the leaders of the pro-Khomeini movement to co-ordinate their efforts to dominate both the Provisional Government and the mass movement. It was a vital centre of organisation, for example, for new bodies such as the *Pasdaran*. The party provided a point of contact for *Pasdaran* commanders, *komiteh* activists, Reconstruction Crusade leaders, workplace loyalists and Khomeini's many supporters among the mullahs. The IRP was the nerve centre for Khomeini's assault on the mass movement.

The party also fulfilled another vital function – it was the mechanism by which Khomeini and his most trusted supporters conducted the battle of ideas with their political rivals.

Since the insurrection the Khomeini group had faced a twin task: it needed to extend its control over the mass movement but could only do so by asserting its influence among the competing factions of the Provisional Government. Here there was opposition from secular and religious rivals. Among the former, the Bazargan group was most influential, representing those areas of Iranian capitalism that remained undamaged by the revolution. These bourgeois nationalists required the re-establishment of private capitalism on the old model but without the excesses of the Pahlavis. They accepted Khomeini's leadership but wanted to run an essentially secular political system.

Bazargan and his supporters had one advantage over the Khomeini group – despite their inability to intervene effectively during the mass strikes they were still operating with a programme of well-established bourgeois nationalist aims. In contrast, the Khomeini faction was improvising strategy. It was not homogeneous and there were many debates and disputes about the way forward – witness the disagreement between Rafsanjani and Khomeini over the vital question of the *komitehs*.

While Khomeini had long had a vision of reforming Iranian society, he and his supporters were far from possessing a formal political programme. They were guided by two closely-connected impulses: the class interests of their most reliable supporters and their own ideological tradition. The group represented class interests substantially different from those of the Bazargan faction. Its closest links were with the petit bourgeoisie – both the traditional layers of the *bazaar* and the technicians of the new industry and middle layers of the state apparatus. In addition, its influence rested not on its status in the old system but on its rise to prominence in the revolutionary events; it was therefore conscious of the need to maintain its relationship with the mass movement.

It was in the IRP that strategy was thrashed out. With Khomeini setting the pace, the party began to elaborate a political programme wwwwhich drew on bourgeois secular models and the Islamic opposition's own traditions. The formulae which emerged also owed something to Khomeini's determination to distinguish his faction from its religious rivals, notably the Islamic People's Republican Party (IPRP) – which favoured a bourgeois nationalist programme with religious colouring – and from the Hojatieh, with its commitment to private capital and its obsessive anti-statism.[8]

The IRP differentiated itself from rivals in the government by identifying closely with the aspirations of the masses. This allowed it to sustain a leading position in the movement, the better to derail it – and to bypass the secular leaders. In line with the position Khomeini had adopted during the strikes of the previous year, much of its rhetoric was therefore radical: it declared itself 'anti-capitalist' and 'anti-imperialist', lavishing praise on the energies of those who had removed the Shah.

At the same time Khomeini insisted that the revolution was to pursue an 'Islamic' course. This meant the consolidation of capitalism and the imposition of a political system deemed to be in accordance with Islamic law. Khomeini was now far more specific about the 'Islamic' character of such a system: it was to be highly centralised and authoritarian – an approach that complemented the instincts of many of Khomeini's closest supporters, especially those petit bourgeois for whom a programme of change from above, instituted by the state, seemed appropriate.

Within these limits the IRP produced a set of ideas which adapted the ideology of the Islamic opposition to the conditions of the revolution. It contained a number of elements: Khomeini's conservative but bitterly anti-Pahlavi attitudes, the rhetoric of Islamic 'radicals', and the language of the mass movement. All these were expressed in the notion which Khomeini made the core of his appeal to the masses: the fundamental social division between the *Mostakberin* (Oppressors) and the *Mostazafin* (Oppressed). Each category was conveniently broad and was not diffentiated internally – but it was made clear that among the *Mostakberin* were the Pahlavis, agents of foreign capitalism, and their supporters. The *Mostazafin* – the workers, peasants and poor, together within their Islamic representatives – were the victims.

While the mass movement was still spreading, this was a flexible approach which could apparently contain the enormous contradiction between Khomeini's influential position within the movement and his determination to destroy that movement. It could express the masses' loathing for the old system – for the Pahlavis and the imperialist powers which had backed them. It could also be used to cast all Khomeini's opponents into the enemy camp. Thus for the IRP those who supported Khomeini were of the Oppressed; those who opposed him were Oppressors – they were allies of the Pahlavis and the dark forces abroad.

This approach allowed the IRP to move with the mass movement while working to head it off. The party called for programmes of economic and political reform and welfare measures to assist the Oppressed. It supported the *komitehs* and even, formally, the *shoras*, declaring that the *Pasdaran* and 'Islamic' workplace bodies would all strengthen the organisations of the Oppressed. The problem of the Oppressors was to be dealt with by the takeover of large enterprises and those operated by 'dependent' capital – a move towards state intervention congenial to many of Khomeini's supporters.[9]

While the IRP appeared to identify with popular aspirations, its rivals in the government were openly hostile to the mass movement. The Bazargan group did not hide its contempt for the the bodies thrown up by the revolution. On the *komitehs*, for example, Bazargan himself was quite specific, arguing that they created 'instability, terror, uneasiness and fear.'[10]. Among Khomeini's religious rivals, the IPRP of Shariatmadari was also critical of the movement from below.

But the most important function of the IRP's analysis of Iranian society was in its approach to the radical elements of the movement. The IRP maintained that it was confronting the undifferentiated 'Oppressor' on behalf of the undifferentiated 'Oppressed'. If the workers' movement had remained intact and if the left had been able to sustain a critique of the IRP's position, the absurdity of such an approach could have been exposed. But as the most advanced sections of the working class were isolated and demoralised the regime became confident: militants who defied the regime's instructions – such as orders to participate in the Crusade for Reconstruction – were declared to be supporters of the *Mostakberin*. With strikes illegal and all energies to be directed to support for the national economy, militants could be characterised as belonging to the Oppressors' camp.

The left made the regime's task easier. The Tudeh repeated Khomeini's analysis as if it were Moscow's own. The guerrilla organisations, still searching for 'progressive' elements in the regime, were partly seduced by it. Indeed, their emphasis on the virtues of the 'national' bourgeoisie appeared to complement Khomeini's. At a time when it should have been sustaining a sharp critique of post-revolutionary society, spelling out the counter-revolutionary character of the regime and the need for the workers' movement to sustain activity in its own right, the left could only provide hopelessly inadequate analyses. Even the best of the guerrillas could do little more than damn *Savak* collaborators and 'dependent' capital – an approach which did not distinguish them from the IRP.

The IRP proved a far more successful agent of class warfare than any of the organisations of the left. It was more determined, more clear-thinking and more effective. It was able to develop a relatively sophisticated approach to the mass movement and to neutralise many potentially hostile elements within it. It was able to improvise new institutions to attack the movement from within as well as to assault it from without. In comparision, the organisations of the left were ineffectual.

The highly-politicised character of the workers' movement had produced an extremely favourable environment for the left – far more favourable, initially, than for Khomeini and his supporters. In the event, even here the IRP won the battle for influence. And the key to its success was not merely its intransigence and inventiveness – it lay in the deficiencies of the left.

Stalinism insisted on the need for a 'democratic' stage of revolution and for a class bloc with 'progressive' elements of the bourgeoisie and petit bourgeoisie. This, it maintained, would allow the establishment of bourgeois freedoms which would open further possibilities for the left. But the 'progressive' elements of the new regime inevitably proved reactionary – and in the face of their offensive, the Tudeh and the guerrillas proved incapable even of fighting for 'democratic' demands. Their attitude to the government's attack on the *shoras*, the women's movement and the national minorities was at best equivocal. As a result, even at this level, they were submerged by the Khomeinist current.

Assef Bayat has pointed out: 'The seizure of power by the ruling clergy was a reflection of a power vacuum in the post-revolutionary state.'[11] This vacuum did not result from the absence of the left but from its inability to offer an independent strategy for the working class. The rise of the IRP – the organisation that filled the vacuum – was a function of the politics of Stalinism.

A base for the regime

During the first nine months of 1979 Khomeini and his supporters laid the basis for a new political order. While they assembled the component parts of a new state apparatus, they presented a 'radical' ideology which seemed to express popular aspirations. This enabled the party to mobilise its supporters against the advanced sections of the mass movement.

Khomeini's most enthusiastic supporters came from the most backward elements of the working class, from the *lumpen* poor and the traditional petit bourgeoisie – groups which had been most completely under the influence of the mosque . They had been particularly active in the street protests but had not been exposed to the influence of workplace organisation. A strong workers' movement – one in which the solidarity of the workplace had an influence beyond the single factory – could have provided an alternative pole of attraction. But as the *shoras* decayed the regime drew the poor behind it.

That such a development was not inevitable is well illustrated by the growth of the unemployed movement in the spring of 1979. Many of those who participated in demonstrations such as that of 1 May, in which employed and unemployed united behind radical demands, had lost their jobs as industry contracted; others were 'marginals' but were drawn along by the momentum of the movement. As the workers moved on to the defensive the unemployed lost confidence and the IRP, under the banner of the Oppressed, became a more powerful pole of attraction.

The position of the urban poor was of great importance. As in many backward countries, recent rural migrants formed a large part of the slum population in most cities, especially Tehran, where the south of the city was synonymous with poverty and suffering. Here the mosque had become increasingly influential.

The urban poor were on the streets from mid-1978 but with the working class exercising decisive political power their weight in the protest movement was reduced. Only in 1979, with the new regime mounting its attack on the working class, did these *lumpen* layers play a vital role. With the Shah gone, Iran had entered a new era – one full of hope, but also characterised by instability and uncertainty. For the most oppressed, the effect was particularly disorienting, and in the absence of a convincing alternative, they renewed their commitment to Islam and the mullahs.

The mullahs' promise of a free and equable society was combined with the notion of the need to return to an ancient model, the *umma* (community) of seventh-century Arabia in which, according to Islamic tradition, the Prophet Muhammed and his followers had lived a simple, fulfilling life, governed by a just, God-given law. This turn to an idealised past was particularly appealing for pauperised masses lacking the confidence of the proletarian collective. The collapse of the secular alternative seemed to confirm the potency of the mullahs' vision and soon it was the poor who were the footsoldiers of Khomeini's *hezbollah* (the Party of God) – an organisation used to attack strikers, leftists and others who were deemed enemies of Khomeini.

It was among the petit bourgeoisie and these *lumpen* layers that the regime laid down its new social base. The revolution had allowed many people to transform their lifestyle – by occupying the property of those who had fled; by ceasing to pay rents and mortgages to landowners and banks; by seizing land; by finding work (and perhaps food and shelter) through the local *komiteh*. Now, as the IRP increased its control, it was able to place its most loyal supporters in new jobs on *komitehs*, among the *Pasdaran*, 'Crusade' organisers and state functionaries. Through the mosque it was able to supply food, shelter, medical help and even work.

This process was just beginning in the months after the insurrection but even at this stage it was clear that the establishment of a new state apparatus was allowing those in power to incorporate thousands of loyalists who came to enjoy a lifestyle unthinkable under the old regime. While the class which had made the revolution was being disarmed, the movement's most backward elements were being placed in positions of privilege.

The IRP wins through

Eight months after the insurrection the IRP was in a position to make a decisive move in the struggle for power. By July it was winning the battle to dominate the government. While Bazargan and his associates still held positions of formal leadership, the party's increasing influence was expressed by the elevation of three party leaders – Rafsanjani, Bahonar and Khamenei – to influential ministerial positions.

But it still faced the problem of controlling the masses. Its chance came as the workers' movement went into decline. By September the number of strikes had declined and the government's campaigns for the *Anjoman-e Islami*, Islamic *shoras* and the Crusade were well under way.

The IRP now took the initiative. On 4 November students backing 'the imam's line' occupied the US embassy and the IRP was quick to mobilise its supporters for mass demonstrations 'against imperialism'. As Khomeini – the *imam* – again cloaked himself in the rhetoric of anti-imperialism, the IRP's opponents fell into disarray. The bourgeois nationalists were outflanked, while, disoriented by the radical tone of Khomeini's statements, even the more intransigent elements on the left (notably the Fedayeen) backed the students.

Khomeini's supporters took full advantage of the confusion. Strikers were damned as agents of the *Mostakberin*; the national minority movements were declared agents of imperialism and Zionism; the left was branded not only as Godless but as traitorous – an accusation to which the nationalistic guerrilla organisations were especially sensitive. The government stepped up the offensive in the factories, pressing for the establishment of Islamic *shoras* and *Anjoman-e Islami*. One result was a rise in the level of workplace struggle but in the absence of any coherent leadership and in the face of the increasingly confident *Pasdaran* the workers were unable to sustain a fightback.

The IRP also took the opportunity to resolve its conflict with the IPRP and increase the pressure on the bourgeois nationalists. When IPRP supporters organised a general strike in Tabriz, mobilising around Shariatmadari's opposition to Khomeini's new constitution, the *Pasdaran* crushed the uprising, while IRP supporters staged huge counter-demonstrations.

The IRP was pushing its governmental opponents to the margins. Although it was 18 months before the bourgeois nationalists could be finally defeated, the Khomeini group had become unstoppable. The IRP brought forward a programme of 'Islamic reform' which removed the few liberties remaining from the revolution. The scene was set for a final push on the workers' movement: *shora* members were physically assaulted and the councils themselves dismissed.

Just twelve months after the insurrection the movement was facing disintegration. The revolution had ended when the *shoras* were forced onto the retreat in summer 1979; now the counter-revolution was in full swing. Khomeini and the IRP had succeeded; despite resistance from the national minorities, armed sections of the left and isolated groups of workers, the consolidation of capitalism was going ahead. The 'riot of democracy' was over and Iran was on the road to a bleak autocracy.

The war

When Iraq ordered its forces into Iran's Khuzistan Province in September 1980 it had two aims: to exploit the confusion of post-revolutionary Iran, weakening its traditional rival for regional dominance, and to direct Iraqis' energies away from opposition activity. The Iranian revolution seemed to present the Baathist rulers of Iraq with a unique opportunity. Since coming to power in 1968 they had hoped to extend their influence into the Gulf region, where the rulers of neighbouring Iran had long held decisive influence. The fall of the Shah and the collapse of the Pahlavi state offered the Baathists their best chance to shift the regional balance of power from Tehran to Baghdad.

Their other aim was to snuff out internal opposition. The Iranian revolution had stimulated hopes for change beyond Iran's boundaries, and in Iraq there had been stirrings among the Shiite population of the south and among Kurds enthused by the re-emergence of the Kurdish movement in Iran. President Saddam Hussein and his fellow Baathists were anxious to neutralise the Iranian movement and to rally Iraqis around the national flag.

The Arab states of the Gulf endorsed Iraq's initiative. They too were anxious about the impact of the Iranian revolution, especially the danger that the large Shiite communities in Kuwait, Saudi Arabia, Bahrain and the United Arab Emirates might obey Khomeini's injunction to overthrow rulers closely tied to the West. Their fears deepened in 1979 after an uprising among Shiites in the Eastern Province of Saudi Arabia, which contained the country's oilfields, the largest sources of mineral wealth in the Middle East.

This also served to draw in the US, which feared for its allies among the kings, emirs and shaikhs who ruled the Gulf states – and for the profits of multinationals such as Exxon and Mobil which had made billions of dollars in the Arab Gulf oilfields. The US thus endorsed the Iraqi initiative. The war was nevertheless not one masterminded by the imperialist powers; it remained a fight launched by a ruthless local ruling class to defend its own interests.[12]

Iraq's offensive was a disaster for Baghdad and a huge boost for the regime in Tehran. Khomeini's first reaction was to use the war as new ammunition for his own offensive against the domestic opposition. Using a combination of sectarianism (the struggle against the treacherous Sunnis – the mainstream current in Islam) and racism (the battle against the Arabs), together with the familiar rhetoric against imperialism, Khomeini called for national unity under his own leadership.

The Tehran regime demanded new sacrifices for the war effort. Workers who resisted demands for increased production or attacks on wages and working conditions were declared Baathist agents or servants of Zionism and imperialism. Worker militants came in for renewed attention from the regime's representatives while the left faced a new offensive in the universities. Meanwhile, the strengthening of the new state apparatus went ahead with increased speed. The army was fully rehabilitated and the volunteer *Baseej* established to fight alongside the *Pasdaran*. Millions of men were mobilised.

Once more, when faced with a question of political principle, the left collapsed. The ingrained nationalism of the major organisations led them to line up behind the regime, calling for a popular front against the national enemy. The Tudeh saw the conflict as a further reason to align with Khomeini's 'anti-imperialism', while the Fedayeen split, one faction (the 'Majority') endorsing the Tudeh position and the other (the 'Minority') calling for support for the government but retaining the right of 'independent' organisation. Meanwhile the 'radicals' of the Mojahedin allied themselves with the liberal wing of the bourgeoisie in government, fully supporting the war effort.

This was the last opportunity for the left to distinguish itself from the regime. It failed to do so, giving Khomeini licence to introduce a policy of repression which within months had become a bloody assault on all those who questioned his authority; later it entrapped even the Tudeh. The left had long since given up its independence; now it paid the full price and by 1983 had been all but destroyed.

The character of the war has been an index of the weakness of the working class and the absence of the left. Despite brief upturns in workers' struggle – notably in 1983 and 1985 – the regime has had its way. Hundreds of thousands of young workers and peasants have been sent to their deaths at the battlefront in efforts to sustain a conflict which has become part of the regime's method of class rule – the war being an integral part of its attempt to assert control; an instrument of repression of the mass of the population.

For Marxists it has been necessary to oppose the war effort – an attitude only modified in 1987 by a change in the character of the conflict dictated by events outside Iran. Then, following US attempts to raise its profile in the region, to confirm its support for the Arab Gulf rulers and renew its commitment to defend the region's oilfields, Washington mobilised an unprecedented show of force against Tehran. It assembled its largest naval force since the Vietnam war and rallied the Arab states in support of Iraq. The US aimed to enforce a peace deal on Tehran which it could present as a victory for the West – a triumph over a Third World state which had been in turmoil since revolution.

Under these circumstances, Marxists argued, success for the US would be seen as a victory for imperialism. In Iran it would delay the day of reckoning with Khomeini and his supporters, benefiting those, such as the monarchists, with the closest links to the West. Abroad, it would strengthen the rulers of the Arab Gulf states and all those opposed to movements like that which removed the Shah. Notwithstanding the reactionary nature of the Khomeini regime, socialists should therefore support Khomeini's military campaign against Iraq and the West, while retaining their complete political independence of the regime.

Khomeini had not, however, become 'anti-imperialist', as those in the Stalinist tradition maintained. Rather, the specific needs of Western imperialism dictated a new offensive against Tehran, in which Marxists could not be neutral. Marxists argued that for an effective struggle against imperialism, workers' rights should be restored; that the campaign against national minorities should cease and the minorities' demands for autonomy should be granted; that only armed mass action could effectively confront the imperialist threat.[13]

A determination to remain independent of the regime is essential. This is especially important in view of Khomeini's success in securing the support of a section of society that the regime claims expresses the backing of the entire Iranian nation.

Demonstrations in favour of the war effort, or to commemorate anniversaries of the movement against the Shah, are presented as national mobilisations which reflect unanimous approval for the regime's policies. In fact, they represent the backing of a section of society which has come to support the regime – those layers which have benefited from the counter-revolution and wish to see the continuation of the present form of class rule.

The Khomeini regime has consolidated capitalism, albeit in modified form. The balance between state and private capital has changed – the state sector is larger under Khomeini, though the regime has made strenuous efforts to tempt private businessmen back to the country. The commercial sector is little changed – indeed many merchants and *bazaaris* boast of profits undreamt of under the Pahlavis, a function of a thriving black economy in which the mullahs and many state functionaries have a stake. It is these sections of society, together with a landlord class somewhat diminished in importance, that determine the regime's priorities.

But the regime has another, vital base – among the newly-privileged functionaries at the lower levels of the bureaucracy, and in the *Pasdaran*, the *Baseej* and the numerous arms of the new state apparatus. Drawn largely from the ranks of the traditional petit bourgeoisie and the urban poor, they have been identified by the regime as its most valued supporters, and rewarded accordingly. They have received homes, salaries and privileges denied the mass of the population and praised as the 'true *hezbollahis*'. These layers have a genuine material interest in the survival of the regime; it is here that Khomeini has rallied support for the war effort and for the repeated mass demonstrations that are said to reflect unanimous backing for the regime.

But the mass of the population remains passively opposed to the regime, to policies which sustain inequality and have introduced new forms of corruption and injustice. The mood among workers is one of sullenness; their movement has not been wholly crushed, and fragments of organisation remain intact, as isolated strikes still show. Eventually, whatever the course of the war, there will be the prospect of a renewed workers' movement and the chance of further radical change. But what will be the response of the left next time round?

5: Lessons of the revolution

THE REVOLUTIONARY POTENTIAL of the Iranian working class is not in doubt. What remains in question is the political tradition of the Iranian left.

The left is fragmented and disoriented. Tens of thousands of activists have abandoned socialist organisations – most have subsided into passivity and even despair. This is not merely a result of the regime's reign of terror – the left's malaise is also a product of its refusal to absorb the lessons of the revolution, its stubborn attachment to ideas which have failed – its inability to explain the fate of the revolutionary movement.

The revolution offers a wealth of lessons. Of these, the most important are those which confirm the Marxist analysis of the capitalist crisis and the strategy for socialist revolution. Earlier they were dealt with in detail; they can now be summarised:

'Exceptionalism': Iran is not a 'special case'. The revolution was a result of processes at work throughout the world system. It was the crisis of Iranian capitalism which brought down the Shah.

Capitalism: The history of Iran is not that of a 'dependent' capitalism, in which Iran has been a mere creature of imperialism. The Iranian bourgeoisie has had its own interest in maintaining the power of capital. The theory of 'dependency' leads to false conclusions about the role of the bourgeoisie and its allies.

The 'progressive' bourgeoisie: The bourgeoisie cannot play a role in the revolutionary transformation of Iranian society. Such change can only be accomplished by the class to which it is implacably hostile – the proletariat. Marxists cannot, therefore, accommodate to sections of the bourgeoisie identified as 'progressive', 'patriotic' or 'anti-imperialist'; or to the petit bourgeoisie, which maintains an interest in the status quo.

The theory of 'stages': There are no 'intermediary' stages between a developing capitalism and a socialist revolution. The idea of a 'democratic' stage results in surrender to the bourgeoisie.

Permanent revolution: Only in a process of permanent revolution can Iranian society be fundamentally changed. In such a process the working class will lead other oppressed groups against the bourgeoisie and those vacillating layers which back capitalism.

Substitutionism: The workers' movement emerges from the needs of the proletariat in struggle. It cannot be engineered by 'revolutionaries' engaged only in abstract propaganda or guerrilla struggle.

The mass strike: Rising workers' struggles produce the mass strike – the workers' principal weapon against capitalism. In such a movement 'economic' and 'political' demands are combined; each stimulates the other as the movement gathers confidence, leading to the rapid politicisation of large numbers of workers.

Workers' councils: In the mass movement workers establish organs of democratic control based on the workplace: in the case of Iran these took the form of strike committees and *shoras*. When such organisation is generalised outside the workplace, organisations representing the advanced sections of the whole class may be formed. Such *soviets* can be the basis for a revolutionary assault on the bourgeois state, which must be smashed. In Iran *shoras* reached a high level of development – but they did not become *soviets*.

The revolutionary party: Under conditions of a rising workers' movement, the role of the revolutionary workers' party is vital. It can generalise political issues, organise the leading militants and eventually lead the assault on the capitalist state. No such party existed in Iran – with a handful of exceptions, 'revolutionaries' were outside the workers' movement.

The struggle for power: With or without *soviets*, the workers' movement cannot be sustained indefinitely. Its survival depends on its ability to confront bourgeois attempts at counter-revolution. In Iran the counter-revolutionary force was led by the clergy and its petit-bourgeois allies.

Revolutionary independence: In such a struggle for power revolutionaries must assert the independent identity of the working class. In the case of Iran the left subsumed the interests of the proletariat below those of a 'progressive' bourgeoisie, directing workers into the camp of the counter-revolution.

Stalinism: Despite a historic opportunity the Iranian left was unable to provide the workers' movement with the leadership it needed. This was a result of its bankrupt political traditions – those of Stalinism. This ideology, alien to the interests of the working class, is also the result of a counter-revolution – that which followed the defeat of the Russian revolution in the 1920s. Its main principles – those of the theory of stages, the need for class blocs, the substitution of other social forces for the working class – dominated the Iranian left. As a result, *the conduct of the left contributed to the victory of the counter-revolution in Iran.*

The debate on the left

In the wake of defeat there has been much discussion on the Iranian left, resulting in numerous splits and re-alignments. Yet there has been almost no re-assessment of the traditions with which the left operated through the 1970s and into the period of revolution. At best, there have been rhetorical denunciations of 'Stalinism', with little understanding of its class basis and its impact on the left worldwide. Indeed, the left remains attached to most of the old formulae. From the major organisations such as the larger factions of the Fedayeen, to the newer splits and grouplets, the old ideas dominate every area of theory.

On capitalism: For the Tudeh Party, the champions of the Stalinist method, the main problem in today's Iran is the country's re-integration into the system of 'dependency' which governed the country before the revolution. The party maintains that Iran is moving back to 'the dependent capitalist system and the renewal of imperialism's economic positions'.[1]

This is a fundamental issue, from which many questions of practice flow. But while most Iranian socialists claim to have distanced themselves from the Tudeh's methods, exactly the same formulation is found in their analyses.

For the Fedayeen Minority the history of Iranian capitalism can only be explained through the theory of dependency. Even in 1987 it argued for an analysis based on the principle of 'the formation of dependent capitalist production relations ... an economic structure developed according to the interests of the imperialist monopolies'.[2] The same approach is found in the analyses of the Communist Party of Iran (CPI), a fusion of Kurdish guerrillas (*Komala*) and the Maoist-influenced *Sahand* group, which claims to have broken decisively with the Stalinist tradition. For the CPI, the modern history of Iran remains that of a 'dependent capitalism': indeed the organisation has developed a new interpretation of 'dependency' to account for the character of Iran's oil-based economy.[3]

On the theory of 'stages': For the Tudeh the analysis which proved such a disaster in 1953 and 1979 is still good enough for the 1980s. The gains of the revolution are seen as those of a 'national and democratic' movement,[4] while the tasks of the masses remain that of securing 'national democratic revolution'.[5]

The Fedayeen Minority has also been insistent that Iran must pass through 'stages' of revolutionary development. It has asserted:

> ... the Iranian proletariat cannot make the socialist revollution its immediate goal ... because of this, the OIPFG [the Fedayeen] sees its primary and immediate task as to overthrow the ruling reactionary regime, the overthrow of imperialist domination and its social base (dependent capitalism), severing all forms of economiç, military and political dependence upon imperialism, and the democratisation of society in order to prepare the conditions for transition to socialism.[6]

The organisation adds: 'Our revolution in this stage cannot be a socialist revolution without an intermediary stage'.[7]

The CPI takes a similar approach:

> ... the conscious proletariat and its communist party cannot embark on an immediately socialist revolution, but is compelled to win, in their first instance, through a victorious democratic revolution, the

most favourable economic and political grounds and preconditions for the ever-tightening of its ranks, for the attraction of an extensive part of workers and toilers under its banner and for its ultimate move towards socialism.[8]

On class blocs: The Tudeh gives a classic definition of the popular front it believes is necessary to advance the revolutionary process in today's Iran:

> The front will comprise workers, peasants, urban petit bourgeoisie and popular intelligentsia, and will endeavour to attract layers of middle and small bourgeoisie which benefit from national and democratic changes.'[9]

The Fedayeen Minority are more cautious over the role of the bourgeoisie but remain certain that the petit bourgeoisie must be part of a front which struggles to take Iran to the 'democratic stage' of the revolution. The organisation argues:

> ... the struggle is mainly taking place around democratic demands, where the workers as well as the lower and middle segments of the petit bourgeoisie in urban and rural areas, as the allies of the proletariat in this stage of the revolution, are being drawn into the arena of struggle.[10]

On substitutionism: The theory of fronts, blocs and alliances itself substitutes non-proletarian forces for the working class but in the case of Iran the guerrilla struggle has been of almost equal importance. On this issue there is little sign that the left has learnt from the errors of the past.

While the Fedayeen Minority claims to be committed to 'proletarian struggle', it defends the practice of the 1970s, which left the organisation a mere onlooker during the events of 1978. Even eight years after the revolution, when the guerilla struggle has been shown to be marginal, the Fedayeen Minority could still argue:

> In February 1971 the Iranian people's Fedayeen Guerrillas, with their correct analysis of the circumstances of Iranian society, correctly attacked the gendarmerie's headquarters at Siakhal, located in the Gilan province, marking a new era in the revolutionary struggle of the Iranian people ... to smash the misconception of

the absolute power of the enemy in the minds of the people and also the misconception of their absolute powerlessness ... The events that followed the Siakhal epic proved the correctness of the Iranian People's Fedayee Guerrillas path.[11]

Meanwhile the notion of guerilla warfare as part of the process of 'liberation' has been extended by some currents. For the CPI, for example, the effort to maintain 'liberated zones' in Kurdistan, based on its *Komoleh* wing, has been central.

The workers' movement: All questions of socialist theory are closely linked; lack of clarity on one issue means confusion on the others. Not surprisingly, the prominence of substitutionist ideas means there have been few attempts to rethink the experience of the working class in struggle. Typically, there is no explanation for the development of the mass strike movement. Often the working class is blamed for pursuing 'economic' rather then 'political' struggles and not advancing to the level of the 'revolutionary vanguard' – that of leftist organisations themselves.

The Fedayeen Minority argues that revolutionary change will be possible when the masses absorb its own 'programme':

> Our victory is possible because there doesn't exist any other revolutionary programme except for the minimum demands of the Iranian proletariat at this stage, which can ensure the rights of the workers, toilers and their conscious and independent struggle towards socialism under the leadership of the conscious proletariat.[12]

While lip-service is paid to the importance of strikes, the actual character of the mass workers' movement is largely ignored. It is significant that in the years since the revolution not one major study of the mass strike movement has appeared from within the organisations of the Iranian left – such work has been left to academics. These organisations have little or nothing to say on the events of 1978 – the development of the mass strike, the strike committees and later the *shoras* – workers' own organisations of struggle.[13] The élitist assumption that workers will line up behind the 'conscious proletariat' reflects a continuing inability to learn from the class or to build socialist organisation through workers' struggles.

Stalinism: None of these organisations can step outside the Stalinist framework – as a result all continue to express illusions in those classes which have created and sustained the Stalinist world view. Little more would be expected from the Tudeh but even in formal terms organisations such as the Fedayeen Minority might be expected to show some caution towards the Russian ruling class and the regimes of the Eastern Bloc.

Despite the experiences of the Iranian revolution and its own split from the pro-Tudeh Fedayeen Majority, the Minority sings the praises of the 'camp of socialist countries against the camp of imperialism'. While the Communist Party of the Soviet Union is regarded as 'revisionist-chauvinist', the Minority considers that 'potential for change and reform' in Russia still exists and it is in Russia, Eastern Europe and South-East Asia that the 'Socialist Camp as the international ally of the proletariat' is most strongly represented. The organisation declares itself hostile to the 'deviationist' lines of 'social-chauvinism', led by the Chinese Communist Party and by Trotskyism.[14]

Much the same formulation is found in the approach of the CPI. While Russia iş said to be under the rule of 'state monopoly capitalism', this is seen as the result of 'Krushchevite revisionism', rather than the work of the counter-revolution which, within ten years of the October revolution, had placed a new state capitalist ruling group in power. For the CPI, the Stalinist world view remains a guide to action – what must be set aside is 'modern revisionism (Krushchevite), 'Three-World' revisionism, 'Euro-Communism' and Trotskyism'.[15]

It is not a little ironic that both the Fedayeen Minority and the CPI should damn 'Trotskyism' as a deviation from the Marxist tradition. Whatever the limitations of Trotskyist organisations in Iran[16] it was Trotsky who, with a handful of surviving Bolsheviks, maintained and developed the Marxist tradition during the years of counter-revolution in Russia, ensuring that a revolutionary socialist current would survive the Stalinist onslaught. In addition, it is only with the insights of Trotsky's own contribution to the Marxist tradition – notably the theory of permanent revolution – that it is possible to understand modern Iranian history and the course of the revolution. The casual dismissal of

'Trotskyism' illustrates how little progress has been made by the Iranian left in its reappraisal of the Stalinist method.

Building a revolutionary socialist party

In the months following the fall of the Shah Iranian workers created a potentially revolutionary situation. Their failure to exploit this historic opportunity was a result of the arrested development of the *shoras* and the successful counter-attack launched by their class enemies.

Had there been an independent revolutionary socialist party, rooted in the working class, the fate of the revolution might have been very different. If such a party, committed to the idea of working class self-activity, had enjoyed the same audience which even the élitist guerrilla organisations attracted, it would have been able to argue for the deepening and widening of workers' self-organisation – most importantly, for the exxtension of the *shoras* in the direction of *soviets*.

Such a workers' party could not have created *soviets* by merely directing workers into new forms of organisation – but in the highly-politicised atmosphere of the period after the insurrection, its members in the *shoras* could have provided a strong pole of attraction for those workers who wanted to extend the councils. They could have argued for organisation across workplaces and industries, for increased control over production and supply, for the establishment of workers' militias, for all those measures which sustain an insurgent movement. They would also have championed the cause of all those fighting to extend their rights – the women's movement, the peasants and the national minority movements.

Depending upon their success – in both the period of mass strike and the period of the *shoras* – they might have been able to raise the question of a direct assault by workers on what remained of the Shah's state – and on the representatives of the petit bourgeoisie who were trying to repair it.

In the event, the left adopted the opposite strategy – arguing for co-operation with elements of the counter-revolution, or at best vacillating when a decisive line was needed. As a result, the new regime was able to strengthen its own weak weapons of class warfare until it could assault the workers' movement from without and from within.

Many Iranian socialists have pleaded that the establishment of a socialist organisation within industry was rendered impossible by the policies of the Shah's regime. But while repression was intense, it did not prevent workers organising. As Bayat, who interviewed scores of industrial militants, points out:

> My study of the strike movement suggests that any collective action was carefully thought out, planned and put into practice. The strike leaders would decide what form of action to take, what kinds of demands to put forward and what tactics to adopt to foil secret police counter-measures. In the early months of the revolutionary upsurge, decisions had to be made in the secret cells which had spontaneously blossomed over the years. The plans would be conveyed to the mass of the workers through trusted connections or through spreading rumours, getting the message across through everybody, and, at the same time, nobody.[17]

There were indeed networks of militants developed over years to resist the employers and the regime. These were unknown to the left because the left was absent from the workplaces. And the left was absent because its theories of revolution dictated that it should be absent. This was a function of the politics of Stalinism.

The lessons of the revolution are stark but such is the grip of the Stalinist world view that most organisations of the Iranian left have progressed little since the events of the revolution. The workers' movement will nevertheless re-organise; new networks will be formed; and in the course of time the regime will come under renewed pressure. Revolutionary socialists will again face the challenge of arguing the way forward. They will only be able to do so if they have broken decisively with the old, bankrupt tradition and adopted the strategies of revolutionary Marxism.

Notes

Chapter 1: CAPITALISM IN IRAN

1. See, for example, Thomas Hodgkin, **The Revolutionary tradition in Islam,** Race and Class, Volume XXI, Winter 1980, pages 221-237. For Hodgkin the Iranian revolution was proof that 'there is an authentic, ancient, but also living revolutionary tradition in Islam.' This, he argues, has much in common with the Marxist tradition: 'Revolutionary Islam seeks to establish a model Islamic community on a worldwide basis, as marxists seek to establish a world socialist commonwealth.' 'Revolutionary' Muslims and Marxists should thus be able to work together to bring political change.

2. For the Fedayeen guerrilla organisation, one of the dominant currents on the Iranian left since the early 1970s, the key period which 'determines the socio-economic infrastructure and political and cultural superstructure of our society' is that since the 1960s. See Bizan Jazani, **Capitalism and Revolution in Iran,** (London 1980), page 77.

3. The *bazaar* has long dominated commerce, finance and artisan production in Iran. The term *bazaaris* includes craftsmen, stalllevels the *bazaar* shades off into the merchant class and the bourgeoisie proper.

4. See N Keddie, **Roots of Revolution** (New York 1981) pages 40-62.

5. W. Floor, **Industrialisation in Iran 1900-1941** (Durham 1984), page 7. Floor argues against the widely-accepted view that large-scale manufacturing industry did not exist in Iran at this period.

6. According to Mangol Bayat, leading ayatollahs pronounced *fatwas* (religious injunctions) in favour of Iranian companies, 'declaring it a holy cause incumbent upon all believers to support "each according to his means" by buying shares'. Bayat, **The Cultural Implications of the Constitutional Revolution,** in E Bosworth and C Hillenbrand, **Qajar Iran** (Edinburgh 1983) page 71.

7. Floor, **Industrialisation,** page 9.

8. W. Floor, **Labour Unions, Law and Conditions in Iran (1900-1941)** (Durham 1985), page 5.

9. Floor, **Labour Unions,** page 6.

10. Floor, **Labour Unions,** page 7.

11. F. Halliday, **Iran: Dictatorship and Democracy** (London 1979), page 177.

12. Floor, **Labour Unions,** pages 12-14.

13. Floor, **Labour Unions,** page 14.

14. The Communist Party of Iran was formed in June 1920. Its membership reflected the upheaval taking place in the small Iranian

working class. According to party estimates, 60 per cent of the rank and file were workers and apprentices, 30 per cent office employees, 7 per cent craftsmen-traders, and 3 per cent intellectuals and soldiers. E. Abrahamian, **Iran Between Two Revolutions** (Princeton 1982), page 115.

15. Floor, **Labour Unions**, page 19.
16. G. Jones, **Banking and Empire in Iran** (Cambridge 1986), page 228.
17. Floor, **Industrialisation**, page 24.
18. Floor, **Industrialisation**, page 24.
19. Floor, **Industrialisation**, pages 30-34.
20. Abrahamian, **Iran Between Two Revolutions**, page 146; Floor **Industrialisation**, page 35.
21. J. Bhahrier, **Economic Development in Iran** (London 1981), page 172.
22. According to Abrahamian (**Iran Between Two Revolutions**, page 147), the total was 170,000, while Floor (**Industrialisation**, page 27), quotes an Iranian estimate of 260,000, which he considers 'on the low side', and a Russian estimate of the total workforce as no less than 525,000. Keddie's suggestion (page 109) that 'there were more workers employed in the oilfields than in all the other industries combined', is clearly wrong. It is this type of error that has fed the notion of Iran as a country in which there was little or no domestic industry.
23. Floor, **Labour Unions**, page 59.
24. Floor, **Industrialisation**, page 30.
25. Floor, **Industrialisation**, page 31.
26. Bhahrier, page 158.
27. Bhahrier, page 159.
28. Abrahamian, **Iran Between Two Revolutions**, page 146.
29. Keddie, page 107.
30. For an explanation of the idea of 'combined and uneven development' and its importance for the theory of permanent revolution, see L Trotsky, **The Permanent Revolution** and **Results and Prospects** (New York 1969), especially chapters 2 and 4.
31. Keddie, page 110.
32. Abrahamian, **Iran Between Two Revolutions**, page 348.
33. Abrahamian, **Iran Between Two Revolutions**, page 284.
34. Abrahamian, **Iran Between Two Revolutions**, page 350.
35. S Zabih, **The Communist Movement in Iran** (Berkeley 1966), page 153.
36. Abrahamian, **Iran Between Two Revolutions**, page 353.
37. Keddie, page 121.
38. Abrahamian, **Iran Between Two Revolutions**, page 362.

39. Keddie, page 133.
40. Abrahamian, **Iran Between Two Revolutions**, page 369.
41. For an account of CIA and British involvement in the coup, see K Roosevelt, **Countercoup: The Struggle for Control of Iran** (New York 1979). Roosevelt described the coup as 'one of the greatest triumphs in America's covert operations'.
42. See, for example, B Nirumand, **Iran: The New Imperialism in action** (New York, 1969). This account of the period views Mossadeq as a 'democrat' leading a mass popular movement; the level of class conflict is simply ignored. In a more recent analysis Moghadam makes the same mistake, passing over this crucial period without a mention of its revolutionary possibilities. Vee Val Moghadam, 'Socialism or anti-imperialism? the Left and Revolution in Iran', in **New Left Review** 166, November-December 1987, pages 7-8.
43. Abrahamian, **Iran Between Two Revolutions**, page 371.
44. Abrahamian, **Iran Between Two Revolutions**, page 357.
45. Abrahamian, **Iran Between Two Revolutions**, page 370.
46. For a full account of the origins and use of the term see H Draper, **Karl Marx's Theory of Revolution,** volume 2 , pages 201-249.
47. For a succinct account of Trotsky's theory see T Cliff, 'Deflected Permanent Revolution', in **International Socialism 1:12,** Spring 1963, reprinted as a pamphlet of the same title (London 1981). Trotsky's original analysis appears in **Permanent Revolution** and **Results and Prospects.**
48. Abrahamian, **Iran Between Two Revolutions**, page 420.
49. Abrahamian, **Iran Between Two Revolutions**, page 422.
50. Bhahrier, page 186.
51. Abrahamian, **Iran Between Two Revolutions**, page 422.
52. Halliday, page 143.
53. Bhahrier, page 192.
54. Halliday, page 176.
55. Halliday, page 143.
56. For an account of the impact of rrecession, see E Abrahamian, Iran: The Political Challenge, in **MERIP Reports** 69, July-August 1978, pages 3-8.
57. Halliday, page 207.
58. Quoted in Halliday, page 208.
59. E Abrahamian, 'Structural Causes of the Iranian Revolution', in **MERIP Report** 87, May 1980, page 25.
60. Hossein Bashiriyah, **The State and Revolution in Iran** (London 1984) page 97.

61. According to Abrahamian, the institution of the *bazaar*, with its 250,000 shopkeepers and traders, reached from the cities into every area of the countryside, with *bazaari* businessmen financing the 430,000 rural workshops which produced carpets, shoes and other craft products. Abrahamian, in **MERIP Report** 87, page 24.
62. The Shah's tame 'Resurgence Party' accompanied inspectors to the *bazaar*, enraging the already hostile shopkeepers and stallholders. Abrahamian, in **MERIP Report** 87, page 25.
63. Halliday, page 154.
64. Halliday, page 151.
65. Abrahamian, **Iran Between Two Revolutions**, page 435.
66. Abrahamian, **Iran Between Two Revolutions**, page 434.
67. Abrahamian, in **MERIP Report** 87, page 22.
68. Assef Bayat, **Workers and revolution in Iran,** (London 1987), page 91.

Chapter 2: REVOLUTION

1. For Keddie, for example, the main groups involved in pressuring the regime were the liberals, students, guerrilla organisations and religious figures: see Keddie, chapter 9.
2. The only account of the revolution to give due weight to these events is Ramy Nima's **The Wrath of Allah** (London 1983), see pages 56-57.
3. Nima, page 57.
4. Shaul Bakhash, **The Reign of the Ayatollahs** (London 1985), page 45.
5. Islam originated in the trading cities of Arabia in the seventh century. It was, essentially, the ideology of the merchant classes of the region, and, as W Montgomery Watt has pointed out, has always been 'deeply penetrated by mercantile terms, not merely in illustrative material, but in the formulation of some of its main doctrines'. See Watt, **Islam and the Integration of Society** (London 1961), page 9. See also M Rodinson, **Islam and Capitalism** (London 1974). Rodinson quotes Torrey on the Islamic concept of the relationship between God and man: 'The mutual relations between God and man are of a strictly commercial nature. Allah is the ideal merchant ... life is a business for gain or loss.' (page 81)
6. Abrahamian, in **MERIP Report** 69, page 4.
7. Abrahamian, in **MERIP Report** 69, page 4.
8. Quoted in Abrahamian, in **MERIP Report** 69, page 4.
9. Karl Marx, 'Contribution to the Critique of Hegel's Philosophy of Right' in **Marx: Early Writings** (London 1975) page 244.
10. D. Hiro, **Iran under the Ayatollahs** (London 1985), page 78.
11. Abrahamian, **Iran Between Two Revolutions**, page 517.
12. Hiro, page 79.

13. Abrahamian, **Iran Between Two Revolutions**, page 518.

14. Hiro, page 99.

15. Rosa Luxemburg, **Ausgewalte Reden und Schriften** (Berlin 1955), pages 201-2; translation from T Cliff, **Rosa Luxemburg** (London 1968), pages 30-31. A different tranlation is to found in Rosa Luxemburg, **The Mass Strike** (Bookmarks, London 1986).

16. For an analysis of the *soviet* during the October Revolution see T Cliff, **Lenin: All Power to the Soviets** (London 1976). On the wave of revolutionary activity in Europe, 1915-1920, see D Gluckstein, **The Western Soviets** (London 1985).

17. Quoted in Terisa Turner, 'Iranian Oilworkers in the 1978-79 Revolution' in P Nore and T Turner, **Oil and Class Struggle** (London 1980), page 282.

18. Turner, pages 282-3.

19. L. Trotsky, **1905** (London 1971), page 123.

20. Bayat, page 96.

21. Turner, page 280.

22. Bayat, page 93.

23. Quoted in Bakhash, page 48.

24. Despite Reza Shah's onslaught on the religious establishment, Khomeini remained silent for 15 years. See Bakhash, pages 20-24. H Algar's, **Islam and Revolution: Writings and Declarations of Imam Khomeini** (Berkeley 1981), also recognises that despite today's carefully-cultivated image of Khomeini as a leader in constant conflict with the Pahlavi state, he was effectively apolitical throughout this period. Algar notes: 'Imam Khomeini's first public statement of a political nature came ... in 1941.' (page 15)

25. Bakhash, page 23.

26. See Bakhash, page 23.

27. Among these, the *Fedayeen-e Islam*, formed in 1946, espoused many of the fundamentalist principles Khomeini later embraced. This group produced a number of activists who became prominent in the pro-Khomeini movement of 1978-79, including Mohammed-Ali Raja'i, president of the Islamic Republic in 1981. See Abrahamian, **Iran Between Two Revolutions**, page 259.

28. Quoted in Bakhash, page 24.

29. Bakhash, page 27.

30. Quoted in Bakhash, page 32.

31. Abrahamian, **Iran Between Two Revolutions**, page 532.

32. Quoted in Algar, page 246. Khomeini, in a declaration on 'The Formation of the Council of the Islamic Revolution', also asserted that the struggle should continue to allow 'the reconstruction of the country for the benefit of the working and oppressed masses'.

33. Quoted in Suroosh Irfani, **Revolutionary Islam in Iran** (London 1983), page 163.
34. Quoted in Bakhash, page 48.
35. Quoted in Irfani, page 163.
36. Bayat, page 131.
37. Bayat, page 151.
38. For a sympathetic account of Shariati's work, see Irfani, pages 116-134. Abrahamian (**Iran Between Two Revolutions**, pages 464-473) gives a much better analysis of Shariati's 'love-hate relationship with Marxism'.
39. Abrahamian, **Iran Between Two Revolutions** , page 456.
40. Quoted in S Zabih, **The Left in Contemporary Iran** (London 1986), page 125.
41. Quoted in Zabih, **The Left**, page 126.
42. Quoted in Zabih, **The Left**, page 129.
43. Zabih, **The Left**, page 130.
44. Quoted in Abrahamian, **Iran Between Two Revolutions**, page 493.
45. Moghadam argues that the Iranian left was ignorant of the discussion of religion and culture initiated by writers such as Shariati during the 1960s and 1970s. But the Fedayeen, for example, were certainly aware of the debate with the Mojahedin, and themselves discussed the role of religion and the clergy. They concluded that 'progressive' mullahs could become 'part of the vanguard of the popular forces' – one reason why the organisation had such difficulty comprehending the role of the religious establishment in the counter-revolution. See Jazani, **Capitalism and Revolution,** pages 62-65, and Moghadam, page 15.

Chapter 3: AFTER THE SHAH

1. The ccis declared that the 118 workplaces and the services were essential to the success of the revolution. Bayat, page 95.
2. Turner, page 280.
3. Bakhash, page 54.
4. Quoted in Bakhash, page 55.
5. Bakhash, pages 55-56.
6. Bayat, page 103.
7. From 215 *Rials* to 567 *Rials* per day. Bayat, page 103.
8. 'Workers' control' in the sense of control over decisions and processes in the workplace, not over decisions in society as a whole.
9. According to Bayat, in December 1978 and February 1979 people took control of a number of cities, especially in the northern Azeri and Caspian provinces, establishing *shoras* to run day-to-day affairs. In the towns of Amol and Sari these were based on representatives of

industrial groups, including teachers, traders and state employees. In Tehran, neighbourhood *shoras* also appeared to organise local administration. However, nowhere was there a direct link between local organisation and workplace organisation. Bayat, page 96.

10. Bayat, page 130.
11. Bayat, page 126.
12. Quoted by M Poya, 'Iran 1979' in C Barker (editor) **Revolutionary Rehearsals** (London 1987), page 147.
13. It was at this stage that enthusiasm for Khomeini and for the nationalisation measures led many members and supporters of the Tudeh Party to take up leading technical and managerial positions. Most were later purged. Moghadam comments that 'one can only shake one's head in bewilderment that such an experienced and established party could have been so wrong.' (Moghadam, page 24). In fact, the Tudeh's liquidation into the new regime was consistent with a practice going back over 40 years.
14. Quoted in Bayat, page 109.
15. Bayat, pages 103-4.
16. Bayat, page 119.
17. Bayat, page 115.
18. Rising oil prices kept the value of Iranian exports high during the early period of the revolution, despite the oilworkers' strikes. In 1977-78 exports of oil and gas were worth $21.2 billion; in 1978-79, $19.3 billion; and in $1979-80, $19.4 billion. Not until 1980-81 did the impact of war reduce revenues to $11.8 billion. It is clear that external factors such as a sudden crisis in the flow of foreign exchange were not responsible for the problems of industry. See L Meyer, 'The Iranian Economy Since the Revolution' in **Aussen Politik** 3/84 (Hamburg), page 303.
19. According to Bayat, between February and July 1979, Iran's national press and the publications of the left showed 287 workplaces raising new demands. (Many other workplaces raising such issues went unnoticed by the press.) Bayat divides these into 'economic' demands, including those for wages, against lockouts, for reduced hours, equal pay and other benefits; and 'radical' demands, including those for the trial of employers and *Savak* agents, the recognition of *shoras*, the victimisation of militants, and the right to strike. These demands were frequently taken up by workplace delegations at demonstrations and rallies, notably those on May Day. See Bayat, pages 103-104.
20. Quoted in Poya, in Barker, page 151.
21. C Goodey, 'Workers' Councils in Iranian Factories' in **MERIP Reports** 88, June 1980, page 6.

22. Bayat, page 146.

23. For a full account of the rise of Russian state capitalism, see T Cliff, **State Capitalism in Russia** (London 1974). For an analysis of the degeneration of the Comintern see D Hallas, **The Comintern** (Bookmarks, London 1985).

24. For a succinct account of the events in China, see Hallas, pages 118-122.

25. See Hallas, pages 139-159.

26. As Abrahamian points out: '... the founding members of the Tudeh were Marxists (and as events later showed, staunch supporters of the Soviet Union) [but] they did not call themselves communists'. Abrahamian **Iran Between Two Revolutions**, page 282.

27. See Abrahamian, **Iran Between Two Revolutions**, page 284.

28. B Jazani, **The Socio-Economic Analysis of a Dependent Capitalist State** (original English translation, published in London by the Iran Committee, no date), page 78.

29. Jazani, **Socio-economic Analysis** pages 89-90.

30. Moghadam argues that 'the new Iranian left developed a distaste for theorising, an impatience at intellectual and analytical work, and a preference for a rather narrowly defined practice.' Moghadam, page 9.

Chapter 4: BEGINNING OF THE END

1. Zabih, **The Left**, pages 88-99 and 135.

2. Zabih, **The Left**, page 137. Fred Halliday maintains that the approach of the left before the establishment of the Khomeini regime was responsible for its subsequent difficulties. He argues against 'its catastrophic stand on liberalism', asserting that an alliance with 'moderate democratic forces' such as Bakhtiar and his supporters could have held the clerical dictatorship at bay. There are two problems with this view. First, Bakhtiar and the liberals were committed to halting the revolution. Unity with such forces would have meant an agreement to dismantle the strike committees and *shoras* – to surrender the independent core of the movement. Second, the liberals and the Khomeini group had a common aim: to re-establish Iranian capitalism, albeit with different priorities. Bakhtiar, appointed by the Shah, would not have balked at using the most repressive methods to control the mass movement. Halliday's approach, like all analyses advocating 'blocs' and 'alliances', fails to grasp the real dynamic of the situation, for under conditions of emerging permanent revolution all sections of the bourgeoisie will retreat to reactionary positions. A wholly independent workers' leadership was necessary to sustain the revolutionary process. See

Halliday, 'The Iranian Revolution and its Implications', in **New Left Review** 166, page 37.

3. Quoted in Bayat, page 133.
4. Quoted in Bakhash, page 57.
5. Quoted in Bakhash, page 58.
6. Quoted in Bakhash, page 59.
7. Bakhash, page 58.
8. For an analysis of the Khomeini group's changing attitudes towards the Hojatieh, see A Vali and S Zubaida, 'Factionalism and political discourse in the Islamic Republic of Iran: The Case of the Hujjatiyeh Society', in **Economy and Science,** volume 14, number 2, May 1985, pages 139-173.
9. Including those of the left, such as the Tudeh and sections of the Fedayeen, who argued for a national, state capitalist strategy.
10. Bakhash, page 57.
11. Bayat, page 134.
12. For an account of contacts between Iraq, the Gulf states and the US see G Nonneman, **Iraq, the Gulf States and the War** (London 1986), page 22. On the US attitude to the war, see J Stork and M Wenger, 'US ready to intervene in Gulf War', in **MERIP Reports** 125/126, July-September 1984, pages 44-48.
13. P Marshall, 'A test of strength', in **Socialist Worker Review,** number 104, December 1987, pages 20-23, looks at the change in the character of the war and the implications for Marxists.

Chapter 5: LESSONS OF THE REVOLUTION

1. **Tudeh News,** number 16, 15 May 1985 (London) page 3.
2. **Iran in Resistance,** number 16, Jan-Feb 1987 (Denver, US), page 8. By 1987, the Fedayeen Minority had split into a number of factions. Their basic political principles remained the same, however.
3. See Unity of Communist Militants, **A Consideration of the Marxist Theory of Crisis and some deductions about Dependent Capitalism** (Manchester 1983). The CPI argues that Iranian oil revenues have long been a form of capital export used by imperialism to ensure that the country remained 'dependent'.
4. **Tudeh News,** number 16, page 1.
5. **Tudeh News,** number 16, page 8.
6. **Kar International,** volume 5, number 1, Fall 1985 (New York) page 13.
7. **Kar International,** volume 5, number 1, page 36.
8. **Programme of the Communist Party** (London 1982), page 15.
9. **Tudeh News,** 23 July 1986, page 7.
10. **Kar International,** volume 5, number 1, page 37.

11. **Iran in Resistance,** number 16, page 10.
12. **Kar International,** volume 5, number 1, page 59.
13. The problem has afflicted most Iranians who comment on the revolution. It can be seen in its most extreme form in Moghadam's recent analysis of the Iranian left. His review of the 1978-79 events contains no reference to the strike movement, the workers' committees or the *shoras*. A notable exception to this tendency is Assef Bayat.
14. **Kar International,** volume 5, number 1, pages 11-12.
15. **Programme of the Communist Party,** page 8.
16. Of the three small Trotskyist groups active during the revolution, two – the HVK and HKE – supported the Khomeini regime. The Third – the HKS – opposed Khomeini, though it has since edged close to an acceptance of the regime's 'anti-imperialism'.
17. Bayat, page 91.

INDEX

Abadan, 15, 16, 41
Abrahamian, Ervand, 35, 118n
Ahmadzadeh, Massoud, 63, 64
Ahwaz, 43, 48
AIOC (Anglo-Iranian Oil Company), 22
Algar, Hamid, 121n
Amazon factory, 91
Amir-Entezam, Abbas, 71
Ansary, Hushang, 48
APOC (Anglo-Persian Oil Company), 16, 17
Azerbaijan, 13, 14, 21
Baath Party (Iraq), 104
Bahonar, Mohammed, 69, 102
Baseej, 107
Basra, 21
Bakhash, Shaul, 54, 70
Bakhtiar, Shahpour, 45
Baluchistan, 73
Bayat, Assef, 36, 51, 52, 59, 74, 77, 81, 100, 116
Bayat, Mangol, 117n
Bazaar, 10, 29, 31, 33, 35, 37, 40, 42, 44, 46, 53, 57, 67, 71, 97, 107, 117n, 123n
Bazargan, Mehdi, 44, 45, 59, 60, 69, 70, 92, 97, 99
Behshahr, 41
Bolshevik Party, 50, 68, 83
Britain, 16, 18, 19, 21, 26
Burujerdi, Ayatollah, 54, 55
Capfi (Centre for the Attraction and Promotion of Foreign Investment), 30
Castro, Fidel, 62
CIA (Central Intelligence Agency), 23, 24
CCFTU (United Central Council of the Unified Trade Unions of Iran), 20
CCIS (Committee for Co-ordination and Investigation of Strikes), 69
Chalus, 19
China, 84
Comintern (Communist International), 82, 83
Communist Party of Iran (CPI), 13, 16, 84, 85, 117n
Communist Party of Iran (*Komola*), 111, 113, 114, 125n
Constitutional Revolution, 12, 38
Dependent Capitalism, 86-87, 111
Engels, Friedrich, 27
Exxon, 104
Fanoos factory, 74
Fedayeen, 45, 62-65, 80, 81, 85, 88, 90, 103, 111, 112, 114
Fedayeen-e Islam, 121n
FLN (Algeria), 62
Floor, Wilhelm, 117n

Founding Council of the All-Iranian Workers' Union, 75
Gilan, 76
Gonbad, 73
Gorgan, 73
Guevara, Che, 62
Halliday, Fred, 124n
Hezbollah, 102, 107
Hojatieh, 97, 125n
Hodgkin, Thomas, 117n
Industry, 10, 15, 17, 18, 30, 51
Iraq, 104-106
Isfahan, 19, 43
IRP (Islamic Republican Party), 93, 96-100, 102
IPRP (Islamic People's Republican Party), 97, 103
Islam, 40, 42, 52, 55, 57, 58, 97
Islamic Associations (*Anjoman-e Islami*), 92, 95, 102, 103
Islamic Republic of Iran, 68, 89, 91
Israel, 55
Jahad-e Sandagi, 95, 99, 102
Jazani, Bizan, 63, 86, 117n
Karaj, 32, 81
Keddie, Nikki, 120n
Kerman, 43
Kermanshah, 20
Khamenei, Ali, 102
Khaneh Kargar, 75, 78
Khomeini, Ayatollah, 29, 39, 43, 44, 45, 52-59, 58, 68, 69, 76, 81, 97, 99, 100, 103
Khurasan, 13
Khuzistan, 16, 20, 21, 22, 43, 73, 76, 104
Komitehs, 92, 93, 94, 95, 96, 98, 102
Komola, 111, 113
Kuomintang, 84
Kurdistan, 13, 21, 73, 104
Land reform, 29
Law of Special Force, 77, 91
Liazonov, 12
Liberation Movement, 60, 65, 67
Luxemburg, Rosa, 47, 48
Mahdavi-Kani, Mohammed-Reza, 93
Majlis, 12, 24, 25
Mao Tse-tung, 63
Marx, Karl, 27, 34, 42
Marxism, 60, 67, 91, 116
Mazanderan, 15, 20
Mobil, 104
Moghadam, Val, 88, 123n, 124n, 126n
Mohsen, Saeed, 65
Moinfar, Ali Akbar, 69
Mojahedin, 45, 65-67, 80, 81, 88, 89